Pretty As A Picture

A Guide to Manners, Poise and Style

by Maria Perniciaro Everding

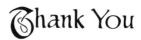hank You

Thank you to our daughter Jodi who was five years old when I was trying to give my program its name; Jodi replied, "Everyone wants to be pretty as a picture." Jodi, who was in sixth grade when *Pretty As A Picture* was published, is now a young woman and still Pretty As A Picture.

Another thank you to Jodi for editing and coauthoring this new edition of *Pretty As A Picture*.

To my husband Gerry who is the love of my life and best friend, thank you.

A hug and kiss to the models: Jodi Everding, Robert and Victoria Perniciaro

I sincerely thank Nancy Ohlemeyer my graphic designer for her expertise, understanding, patience and great sense of humor.

To the consultants of the Etiquette Institute who teach my classes, I can honestly say I wouldn't be where I am without you. Thank you for all you do for me.

And most importantly, I thank all of our *Pretty As A Picture* graduates. You have made my dream a reality.

PRETTY AS A PICTURE, A Guide to Manners, Poise and Appearance

Copyright © 1986 & 1999 by Maria Perniciaro Everding

Printed in the United States of America.   Second edition

Library of Congress Card Number 86-82942
ISBN 0-9617665-0-6

Dedication

With "love and gratitude" I dedicate this new *Pretty As A Picture* book to the loving memory of my parents, Vic and Rose Perniciaro, who were always there for me with their love, support, encouragement and help. They thrilled in seeing the *Pretty As A Picture* book become a reality in 1986.

Contents

Let's Talk

What makes you feel really good about yourself? Is it getting an "A" on a test you studied long and hard to pass? How about going shopping and buying a new outfit or game? Or, is it when you do something to make someone else happy? Maybe it's when your parents tell you how proud they are of you. All of these things *are* important and would make anyone feel good; however, you have the right to feel good about yourself all of the time, and with confidence, you will.

When you're confident, you have an inner fire and outer glow. Everyone likes to be around you because you are a positive, upbeat person. You feel good about yourself. With confidence, you can do anything you put your mind to.

A confident person has good manners, which are kind, polite ways to act while with other people. Don't worry about the rules of etiquette. Use them as guidelines. However, without rules of etiquette (the proper ways to behave), life could be chaotic or in some situations even barbaric. If you follow the *Golden Rule*, you will always be correct.

I wrote this book for you because you are at an *in between* time in your life. In between what, you might ask. In between Barbie dolls and boys...you've outgrown the cute little girl stage; however, you're not a teenager yet. You probably feel like you're out in left field with all sorts of strange things happening to you.

Your body is changing—maybe faster, maybe slower than your best friend's. You feel weird. Your mother won't let you wear makeup, but *everyone else is*...another way of feeling different. Some of your classmates are even considering boy-girl parties. Maybe you're still not interested in the opposite sex. You wonder why. You try to be noticed or try to be as popular as others and you can't figure out what's wrong. You're not alone. These are normal feelings.

As you read through this book, you will learn how to be at ease with your peers, with adults and most importantly with yourself. You will learn the proper things to do and say in all situations. You will become confident, poised and feel good about yourself. You are as good as anybody and better than nobody.

I am so glad you have this book. You'll find it easy to use and fun to read. So, what are you waiting for? Turn the page and get started!

CHAPTER ONE

Hello, How Do You Do

Introductions

Do you like to make introductions? Most people don't because they really don't know what to say and are afraid of saying the wrong thing. If you, too, are unsure or nervous about introductions, you're in the right place because this chapter will help you overcome those feelings. Keep reading!

What is an introduction? It's a very special meeting—it's the sharing of friends. Introductions can be fun and might be the start of lifetime friendships.

The Rules!

Mention the name of the person to whom you're showing honor first. That means mention people with titles (doctors, lawyers, teachers, etc.) or older people. (It used to be ladies first.)

Now Forget The Rules

It's better to make the introduction, right or wrong, than to ignore the whole situation. Besides, most people don't really care (or notice) whose name is mentioned first.

- "Anybody who is somebody looks down on nobody."

Tips

- If possible, use first and last names. Otherwise first names only will do it.
- If you forget someone's name, just say, "I'm sorry, but I've forgotten your name." The person will fill you in, and then you can continue.
- Speak slowly and clearly. It's hard to understand someone who mumbles.
- Mention something that you know about each person. For example, both are on swim teams, play musical instruments, or like to read.
- Don't start introductions with a command such as "Meet my friend" or "Shake hands with." Use "This is" instead.
- Smile. An introduction is incomplete without a smile!

Specifically Speaking

When introducing a friend to your mother:

- ☞ "Mom, this is Beth Bright. ☞ Beth, this is my mother."

  Because you didn't mention your mom's last name, Beth assumes that it is the same as yours and calls her Mrs. Samelastname.

You don't need to mention your mother's last name unless it is different from yours.

- ☞ Mom, this is Beth Bright. ☞ Beth, this is my mother, Mrs. Jones."

  Now Beth knows to call your mother Mrs. Jones.
  (If she doesn't, let her borrow this book to read.)

When introducing a friends' parents or your parents' friends:

- ☞ Call your friends' parents "Mr. & Mrs."

  Your parents' friends, however, may want you to call them by another name such as "Aunt", "Uncle", "Tootsie", or whatever. This is their decision and your parents' decision, not yours. If not, refer to them as "Mr.", "Mrs.", "Miss", or "Ms." This is also how you would introduce them to someone else.

FYI:

- ☞ A married woman is called "Mrs."
- ☞ A single girl may be called "Miss" or "Ms."
- ☞ In the business world (this is for future reference) "Ms." is the proper title for all women.

When introducing family members:

State their relationship.

- ☞ "This is my sister, Glenda Marks," -or-
- ☞ "This is my stepmother, Mrs. Smith."

Which is most important?
- ❏ *showing respect*
- ❏ *a smile*
- ❏ *being pleasant*
- ❏ *all of the above*

When introducing persons with titles:

Any person with a title should be referred to by his or her title. This means the specific title is said first followed by the person's name. A rundown of titles is as follows:

- "Mr. President" (President of the United States, should you be so lucky)
- "Doctor"
- "Rabbi"
- "Father" (Catholic Priest)
- "Sister" (Catholic Nun)
- "Your Holiness" (Pope)
- "Bishop"
- "Cantor"
- "Governor"
- "Mayor"
- "The Honorable" (other government officials)
- "Your Majesty" (King or Queen)
- "Your Royal Highness" (Prince or Princess)

How Do You Do?

This is what you say when someone is introduced to you. There's no need to answer this question, but if you insist "Just fine, thank you" is okay.

Avoid saying "Pleased to meet you," or "Delighted." They sound insincere.

What else? If you've heard nice things about the person, say so. Say how happy you are to meet him, but ONLY if you mean it.

- "Susie has told me so much about you. I am so happy to meet you." -or-
- "I have really been looking forward to meeting you."

Pardon Me

If a person's name is not stated clearly, ask to have it repeated. Say,

- "I'm sorry, what is your name?" -or-
- "Excuse me, I didn't hear your name."

A Person You Have Just Met

Refer to the person the way she is introduced to you:

- ➥ "Miss Smith, this is my cousin Elizabeth Jones. ➥ Elizabeth, this is my teacher, Miss Smith."

Elizabeth calls your teacher "Miss Smith," and Miss Smith calls your cousin "Elizabeth." Simple!

Shaking Hands

Hand shaking is always appropriate. A kind person eagerly extends a hand to shake. If you're not fast enough to extend your hand first, then accept a handshake from someone else. It's obvious if your hands are full and not free for the shaking, so just smile and nod.

When you shake hands, look the person directly in the eye and smile as you grasp his hand firmly (without breaking any fingers, though).

On the other hand, don't give a wimpy, "wet fish" handshake by barely grasping the other person's hand. It makes the other person feel like he's holding a wet fish. Yuk.

Practice! Find someone in your home right now and shake hands. Get feedback from her: How was the handshake—too firm, too limp, or just right? And what about the smile? (Beautiful, of course.)

It's awkward to shake hands with someone your own age, but always shake hands with an older person. (It's a great way to get brownie points!)

Make sure that you don't reach across anyone when extending your hand.

Stand Up

It's a form of respect to stand whenever an older person (including your parents) enters the room. After all, don't you greet someone when they come in?

You also stand when the host, hostess, or honored guest enters the room. When you stay seated, it says, "Hey you're not very important." When you stand, look the person directly in the eye — you are telling that person that he is important and so are you.

What's in a Name?

Plenty—everyone loves to be called by her correct name. When you remember someone's name it makes her feel special. She knows you care and will remember you for your thoughtfulness. Remembering names takes practice, though...

Have you ever been talking to someone and suddenly you can't remember his name? Your mind's gone completely blank and you're hoping that you won't have to use his name. You're forced to wait for him to look at you before you speak.

Better learn a few tricks of the trade:

How to remember a name:
- ❑ *concentrate!*
- ❑ *repeat it aloud*
- ❑ *repeat silently*
- ❑ *associate with face*
- ❑ *think of someone else with same name*

- ☛ Concentrate. Pay attention to what is being said.
- ☛ Add the person's name to the end of your "How do you do."
- ☛ Repeat the name two or three times silently.
- ☛ Use association.

Put the name with the face. (For example, Mrs. Bloomeyer has blue eyes, Mr. Whalen is as big as one, or Sandy is visiting from Florida.) Or, choose something the person is wearing and imprint it in your mind. Try thinking of someone you already know with the same name and compare the two persons.

Use whichever method works for you, because don't you feel good when someone remembers you by name?

Forgot a Name?

So back to that sticky situation when someone approaches you and you can't remember her name. What do you do? Be honest. Admit that you can't remember the name.

- ☛ Say: "I'm sorry, I've forgotten your name," -or-
- ☛ "I know your face, but I can't remember your name."

An alternative (in case you don't want to admit you have forgotten) is to reintroduce yourself:

- ☛ "I'm Joe. We met at the last hockey game."

    The other person will automatically respond with his name. Whew! This saves everyone.

Do You Remember Me?

Don't even ask. You just set yourself up to hear the answer: "No." Instead, reintroduce yourself.

At Any Gathering...

Walk up to any group or person and introduce yourself. Add something about yourself.

- ☞ "Hi, I'm Susan. I play soccer with Tricia," -or-
- ☞ "Welcome to Wood Hollow, I'm Mark. We have English together."

If you are the host or hostess, don't stop the entire party to introduce a newcomer. (What a way to make someone new feel even more awkward!) Instead, introduce her to a small group of people at a time.

When you leave the party, tell your new acquaintances how much you enjoyed meeting or being with them:

- ☞ "I enjoyed talking with you, John," -or-
- ☞ "Can't wait until we get together again, Kim."

Practice. Be eager to make introductions. Learn to enjoy sharing friends. Most importantly, make an introduction, right or wrong, rather than ignore the person or situation.

Which is worse?
❑ *making an introduction incorrectly*
❑ *not making an introduction at all*

Conversation

What's Up?

Do you like to talk? Most people do, but there's an art to starting a conversation and keeping it going that you must develop. There is a difference between just talking and having a conversation. Anyone can talk and say nothing, but conversation is an exchange of ideas. Think of it as a two-way street (not a one-way street with you doing all of the talking).

Ask Questions

You can always depend on the weather to get a conversation started:

- ☛ "Can you believe this weather?"
- ☛ "Aren't we having a beautiful spring?"

Which are do's and which are don'ts?
- ❑ *weather*
- ❑ *personal questions*
- ❑ *what…*
- ❑ *where…*
- ❑ *how…*
- ❑ *yes/no answers*

Avoid questions that are personal or could hurt someone's feelings. Don't ask:

- ☛ "Why is your sister so fat?"
- ☛ "How much money does your dad make?"

If someone asks you a personal question, say:

- ☛ "I really don't know"
- ☛ "That doesn't concern me"
- ☛ "I really don't want to discuss it."

Here's a poem that will help you start and carry on a conversation:

- ☛ I know six handy serving men.
  They taught me all I knew.
  Their names are WHAT and WHY and WHEN
  And HOW and WHERE and WHO.

Ask questions beginning with these words. Think of "what, when, where, why, and how" as conversation crutches. (Lean on them!) You will never be at a loss for things to talk about with them. Choose any subject. For example, vacation.

- ☛ WHAT   What are you going to do on your vacation?
- ☛ WHY   Why did you choose Florida?
- ☛ WHEN   When are you leaving?
- ☛ HOW   How are you getting there?
- ☛ WHERE   Where are you staying?
- ☛ WHO   Who's going with you?

Listen to the answers with interest. You're not playing 20 questions or asking question after question just to hear yourself talk.

Answer with More Than "Yes" or "No"

A yes-and-no person doesn't leave an opening for a good conversation. Say something after you say "yes" or "no":

- ☛ "Yes, we had a great time. We went..."
- ☛ "No, I don't have any brothers or sisters, but I have a dog."

Lend an Ear

One secret to being a good conversationalist is to be a good listener. It's also a great way to learn about people, places, and things... but it's difficult to do. Everyone loves to talk to someone whose mind is not drifting somewhere far away (out in space?) If you're eager to listen, people will be eager to talk to you.

Know when to listen (when others are talking) and when to talk (when others are listening). This is the key to becoming a good conversationalist.

But How Co—Don't Interrupt

Interrupting someone is as rude as shoving them (and mid-sentence, no less). Even though what you have to say is important, you should wait until someone is finished speaking before you start.

If you MUST interrupt (and it better be good) say:

☛ "Excuse me..."

☛ "I'm sorry to interrupt, but..."

Try not to finish someone else's sentence. It's impolite and irritating.

Tone It Down

Keep the tone of your voice low and soft. If you have a squeaky or high- pitched voice, practice reading something dull and boring out loud to try to lower your pitch.

If your voice is dull and flat (monotone), you can pep it up by reading nursery rhymes out loud with lots of exaggeration. (And young children will come from across your neighborhood to listen!)

Attention, Please

When someone asks for your attention, stop what you are doing and give her your attention.

On the other hand, when your attention is not necessary (For example, when your mother has a friend over and they sit down to talk), graciously disappear. Find something else to do before someone gives you his suggestions!

Eye Contact

Look directly into the other person's eyes. It makes her feel important and interesting, and let's her know that she has your complete attention. (If what she's saying isn't so interesting, however, mum's the word.) Don't gaze around the room or tap your feet or fingers no matter how tired you are of hearing about how the federal budget can be balanced or how the theory of relativity applies to everyday life.

Compliments

You can always find something nice to say about or to someone. If you like someone's shoes, dress, jewelry, etc., say so.

Compliment a friend when he scores high on a test or when she hits a home run for the softball team (even if you struck out). They'll feel great, and so will you! You'll become more popular just by looking for (and finding) the good in others.

Thank You

A compliment ("You're hair looks great.") is a gift, so respond with "thank you." If you disagree with the compliment ("Oh, I hate it. What a terrible haircut.") you insult the person's taste. Accept compliments graciously and enjoy the good feeling.

You Instead of I

Make you the most important word in your vocabulary, and put I at the end of your list. You can probably pick out the people who've not learned this valuable lesson. They're the ones who are always saying "I" this and "I" that. They are bossy, boring, and not very popular... and they are certainly not interested in *you*.

Group Conversation

A good rule to follow is don't speak twice until everyone has spoken once. There's no need to get out a scorecard, but just don't monopolize the conversation. What you have to say is important, but remember the two-way street!

How well do you:
- *pay attention*
- *make eye contact*
- *compliment*
- *say 'thank you'*
- *say 'you' not 'I'*
- *take turns talking*
- *tell the truth*

Respect Others' Opinions

Try to avoid arguments; no one ever seems to win, and hurt feelings often result. Say:

- "I understand how you feel. I guess we just have different opinions."

Then drop it. (This can be difficult.) Can you think of someone who prefers to argue? Do they ever win?

Tact is the ability to close your mouth before someone else wants to!

Tell the Truth

Someone who lies will eventually get caught. If someone lies to you, he'll also lie about you. Honesty is the best policy. (Always was and always will be.)

Bragging Is Showing Off in Words

No one likes a show off. When you have something to toot your horn about, let others beep it for you. A show off says: "Here I am, look at me, I am so wonderful."

Don't Snitch

Whatever someone does will surely be found out sooner or later without your help. No one likes a tattler.

Shhh!

Save whispering and telling secrets for private times with a friend. If you whisper in front of someone else, she'll think that you're talking about her. (It's a natural reaction.) Whispering in front of others just leaves them out and makes them feel bad—how would you feel?

Zip It Up!

When someone trusts you with a secret, keep your mouth shut. Trust is what friendship is all about.

Bite Your Tongue

How often do you:
- ☐ *show off*
- ☐ *tattle*
- ☐ *tell secrets*
- ☐ *gossip*
- ☐ *criticize*
- ☐ *belittle others*
- ☐ *complain*
- ☐ *point*

If you're tempted to gossip, bite your tongue. The less you gossip, the fewer the unkind things that someone can say about you.

Maybe someone is trying to get you to talk about someone else. Respond with:

- ☛ "I hear what you say, but I like her."
- ☛ "She's a really nice person when you get to know her."

I Told You So

After making a mistake or causing a disaster, the culprit does not have to be reminded that you, in your infinite wisdom, "told her so." She remembers where she heard it and probably feels bad enough already.

Don't Belittle Anyone

Never make fun of someone who may be different in any way. People with mental or physical limitations deserve your respect and understanding. And it's a mistake to laugh at someone who's made one.

You are as good as anybody, but better than no one! This applies to telling ethnic jokes or making fun of someone's dialect or accent.

Oh, Poor Me!

Hard to believe, but half of the people you tell your problems to aren't really listening. Save your breath.

And save your pouting and sourpussing for when no one else's around. Your problem is probably minor compared to the situations of many other people in this world. And it won't seem nearly as bad in a day or two.

Pointing Is Rude

When you point your index finger at someone, you have three fingers pointing back at you!

Please and Thank You

Always use these words. I know you've heard this a million times, but it shows that you're respectful of others.

Please and thank you will never wear out. *Please* encourages people to help you; and no one ever gets tired of hearing *thank you*, which sounds better than *thanks* (although *thanks* is better than nothing).

Practice Speaking

Be aware of proper enunciation and pronunciation. If you don't know how to pronounce a word properly, look it up in the dictionary. Make a note of it, and work it into your vocabulary.

Don't grunt or make sounds for words. (We worked out way up the evolutionary ladder for a reason.)

Don't slur or mumble. Make sure that you say:

- "Did you," not "Didja"
- "For," instead of "Fer"
- "Ladies and Gentlemen," not "Ladiesandgentlemen"
- "It's not," for "Itsnot"
- "Yes," instead of "Yeah"
- "What," instead of "Huh"

Which is correct?
- ❏ *thank you*
- ❏ *yeah*
- ❏ *please*
- ❏ *uh-huh*
- ❏ *yes ma'am*
- ❏ *it's like you know*

And don't drop the endings of going ("goin'") and doing ("doin'"). The last sound in a word is just as important as the first.

Read tongue twisters to train yourself to speak more slowly. If you go too fast, your tongue will get twisted... and who knows what you'll say?

Here are a few for practice:

- ☛ The swan swam over the sea. Swim, swan, swim. The swan swam back again. Well swum, swan.
- ☛ Betty Bright burned a basket of brown baking biscuits.
- ☛ Theophilus Thistle, the successful thistle sifter, sifted a sieve full of unsifted thistles and thrust three thousand thistles through the thick of the thumb. Success to all successful thistle sifters!
- ☛ How much wood would a woodchuck chuck, if a woodchuck could chuck wood? A woodchuck would chuck all the wood, if a woodchuck only could.

Don't Correct Anyone

Unless you're a teacher, teaching a class, it's not your place to correct someone who uses the wrong word or mispronounces a word. Instead, continue using or pronouncing the word correctly.

Uh, Like, Speech Tics, You Know

A speech tic is an annoying habit that you should train yourself to avoid. Speech tics are the *you knows*, the *OKs*, the *uhs*, and so on, that people slip into their speech without knowing. Most people don't realize that they have a speech tic until they actually hear themselves speak.

Try it: sometime record your conversation on the phone with a friend. Play back the tape and listen for all the *uhs* and *likes*. You'll be amazed at how many you hear.

So how do you break this habit? Now that you're aware of your speech tic, every time you catch yourself using one, stop and begin your sentence again.

Now that you're on to the nasty little speech tics in your sentences, you'll probably catch them popping out of your friends' mouths, too. But unless you want to change these friends into enemies, don't nag them about their speech tics. Let your good speech habits rub off on them.

14

You Know What I Mean?

No not exactly... Instead of asking something this, just *say exactly what you mean.*

Don't use the word *like* to say what you mean. "...Or something like that," doesn't clue anyone in — something like *what?*

Have you ever heard someone say, "Whatchamacallit," or "Where's that thing from whatsherface?" Everything has a name. It'd be great if we could read each other's minds when this happens, but because we can't, it's better to say what you mean. (Stop and think for a minute until the name of "that thing" comes to mind.)

Learn From Your Elders

Be especially courteous and respectful when talking to older people.

It's hard to imagine, but they were young like you. Ask them their interests: bringing up grandchildren will get the ball rolling, and then you can move onto golf, favorite recipes, family traditions, and holidays. You can learn a lot from someone who has lived a long time, and she in turn will appreciate your interest and be eager to share fascinating thoughts and memories with you.

Silence is Golden

It is better to talk too little than too much. A "bore" will talk forever and ever and say nothing.

Think of the word H-E-L-P and how it can help you.

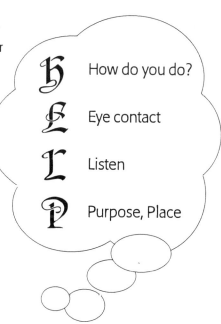

H — How do you do?

E — Eye contact

L — Listen

P — Purpose, Place

Telephone Tactics

You're home alone. You just got in the bathtub when the telephone rings. You get out (and aren't too happy about it) and answer the telephone with a crabby tone.

You're being grounded and you're angry. The telephone rings. You answer it with a harsh, irritated voice.

Or, you had a great day at school. You got an A on your math test and won your soccer game. The telephone rings. You answer it not with just a pleasant voice, but with a warm, happy, singing tone.

The way you answer the telephone gives a good or bad impression to the person on the other end. Granted, some people who call may know that you usually have a charming personality and assume that you're just having a bad day. But you can't take that chance.

Answer the telephone (within three rings if possible) with a smile in your voice. Forget the grunts and barks and don't try to be silly.

Hello?

What do you say when you answer the phone? If your parents want you to answer the telephone a certain way, you'd better get it down. Otherwise, the best way to answer the telephone is with a friendly, "Hello."

If the call is for someone else and that person is home, say, "Just a moment please." Scratch, "Yeah, hang on" from your vocabulary. (What do you want someone to hold onto? [This is a pet peeve of mine.])

Gently put the receiver down and go get the person. *Tell* (don't *yell* to) him that he has a phone call. If your house is too large to run to the other end to get the person (I've heard this excuse before), you'd better put some skates on, because you may not yell!

If the call is for someone who's not home or is unavailable, then say, "I'm sorry, but my dad is not available right now. May I take a message or have him return your call?" (It's a good policy never to tell a stranger your parents aren't home.)

Repeat the message or number as you write it down, and then say, "Goodbye" (not "goombye" or "baa" or "bye bye"), and gently hang up the receiver.

Now it's your responsibility to see that whomever the call was for gets the message. (Write it down!)

Making a Call

Always state your name first when calling someone. Say:

- ☛ "Hi, Mrs. Berg, this is Angie. May I please speak to Liz?" -or-
- ☛ "This is Sue Jones, May I please speak to Alison?"

If you know Mrs. Berg, ask her how she is or what's new before you ask to speak with Liz.

If Liz is not home, leave your message and say "thank you" before you hang up the receiver (gently).

It's none of your business where Liz might have gone, so don't ask. Other questions such as "Who is Craig with" are also intrusive.

Have a specific reason to call someone. Say what you have to say, then say your goodbyes. If you have plenty to say, ask the other person first: "Do you have a few minutes to talk?"

Maybe your friend is talkative and you're unable to spend time on the telephone being a good listener. Say:

- ☛ "I'm really sorry, but I can't talk right now. I still have homework to do." -or-
- ☛ "I'm sorry; I'm really distracted right now. May I call you back?" (And do.)

Return Your Calls

If someone cares enough to call you, but you're unable to take the call, return it as soon as possible. No excuses.

Wrong Number

You should never give your telephone number to a caller. A nice reply to: "What number is this?" is:

- ☛ "It's the number you dialed."

Someone who apologizes for dialing incorrectly should be answered with, "That's OK."

Maybe you've reached the wrong number (heaven forbid). Simply apologize:

- ☛ "I'm sorry, I must have dialed incorrectly."

Caller ID

If you have caller ID, avoid picking up the phone and stating the person's name, "Hi, Judy." This is annoying. Answer in the usual way - "hello" with a smile in your voice. Besides no one has to know you have caller ID.

Answering Machines/Voice Mail

When the "machine" is on duty, just speak into the telephone slowly and clearly. It is difficult to try to decipher a garbled message. Say what you have to say and gently put the receiver down.

There are some pretty funny recorded messages. Just chuckle if you should get one, but don't hang up without leaving your message. Even though you leave a message, be sure to call back, because you never really know if the person got your message.

Call Waiting

When you're on the telephone and a call comes through for one of your parents, you must get off the telephone IMMEDIATELY. What you should say is, "Just a moment please, I'll get her." Someday when you're an adult you'll have the same privilege.

Should another friend call, while you're on the line, tell the second caller that you're on the other line and ask if you may call back. Your obligation is always to the first caller.

Beepers

Unless you're a doctor on call, you don't need a beeper. *If* you should have a beeper, make sure it's on vibrator when you're with others.

Cellular Phones

There's a time and a place for cellular phones. You should go to a lobby or someplace away from others, if you have to use your cell phone. If you are calling someone's cell phone, remember they are paying for the call, so be brief. Always state your name first.

Phone Time

You surely know the telephone rules and regulations in your house. Let them be your guide; don't hang on the telephone for hours—it's a waste of valuable time.

Speaking of wasting time, don't leave someone waiting on the telephone while you changing the CD or put your dog out. If you *must* leave the telephone, then suggest that you'll call the other person back.

If you're at someone's home, ask for permission to use the phone, and then make your conversation brief.

Don't answer the telephone at someone else's home unless you're asked to do so.

Babysitting

When you're babysitting, only use the telephone with the parents' permission, and then, only after the children are asleep. Never give out the telephone number to your friends.

Community Conversation

When someone calls to talk to you, avoid bringing everyone else in the room into the conversation. That person on the phone called to talk to you, not to "hold on" while other family members say what they think.

Reverse the situation. When someone else is on the phone, avoid interrupting or trying to add to their conversation. This is also very annoying.

Eavesdropping

Don't do it. Listening to someone's conversation from another extension is definitely impolite and should never be done.

Prank Calls

Don't use the telephone to prank people. With caller ID and call return, you'll probably get a call right back.

If you answer and it's a prank call, don't play detective by trying to find out who it is. Hang up.

Lights, Camera, Action

And... you're on! It's your turn to speak before an audience. There's a big difference between talking from a seated position and standing before an audience to give a speech. No need to be afraid, however.

An audience can be any group, such as your classmates, church group, club, or Boy Scout troop.

Before you take center stage, here are a few helpful suggestions:

- ☛ Be the first to give a speech, if you have a choice in the matter. Once you're finished, you can sit back, relax and listen to everyone else.

- ☛ The most common speech problem is articulation. Some people call it enunciation or diction, but whichever word you choose, say it clearly because it means the way that you form your words, sounds, and syllables.

- ☛ Good speech is a talent you can develop.

- ☛ Know your subject. This doesn't mean that you necessarily have to have your speech memorized.

- ☛ Practice at home, before a full-length mirror. Parents expect perfection, so it might be better to keep them in suspense until you make the big speech.

- ☛ Take several deep, deep breaths before you get up to speak. Squeeze your hands together and release to relieve some of the tension. You won't get rid of your butterflies, just put them in order.

- ☛ If you feel better with tons of notes, that's OK, but don't just read from them or hold and shuffle them in front of your face.

- ☛ Stand on both feet with your weight evenly distributed.

- Avoid clutching the microphone or podium for support — you won't fall!

- Don't look for a familiar face in the audience. This will surely make you lose your train of thought. However, it may help to choose one person—any person — to look at and smile.

- Wear a new outfit or something special. The most important thing you wear is your expression, so make sure it fits the speech.

- To get your audience involved, ask them a question: "How do you feel about..."

- If you are a natural comedian, go with it! If you're not, don't try to be life of the podium. Your humor will go over like a lead balloon!

- Believe in yourself. You have something to offer and something interesting to say. Everyone wants to hear you.

- If you totally forget everything right in the middle of your speech — stop. Avoid uh, uh, uh (this is a dead give away). Be silent. Think of what you were going to say. Look at your audience; they'll be sitting on the edges of their seats wondering if you're going to call on someone or what earth-shattering statement you're about to make. If nothing comes to you, and you can end your speech, do so.

- A positive exit is a must. Be sincere. You might say something like:

  > "Thank you. I've enjoyed being with you today."
  > If you can't get through that, simply say: "Thank you" and smile!

The nicest gift you can give a speaker is your attention.

Don't be afraid to make a speech:
❑ *relax*
❑ *practice*
❑ *use notes*
❑ *smile*
❑ *ask questions*
❑ *be yourself*
❑ *be sincere*

CHAPTER TWO

Going Places, Doing Things

Attending the Theater or a Concert

At the theater or at a concert, the artists are performing live, unlike the movies where a film is being shown, so the basic rules of conduct at any public place of live entertainment are the same.

Don't draw attention to yourself by being noisy or acting silly. You'll receive the right kind of attention when your manners are what they should be.

Be on Time

It's rude to be late. At a live performance, you may be asked to wait in the lobby until there is an intermission or an appropriate time to take your seat.

Tickets

If you are the hostess, (a birthday party at the theater can be fun) you'll hand the tickets to the ticket taker. Then step aside to let your guest(s) go in first.

Hand the ticket stubs to the usher at the end of the aisle. This usher will hand you a program.

Taking Your Seats

Follow the usher to the seats. You may only switch seats with someone after you are seated. Don't stand in the aisle trying to figure out who is going to sit where.

Face the stage as you pass in front of the people already seated in your row. (In Europe, it's just the opposite.) Keep your body as close to the backs of the seats you are facing and be careful not to drag anything (such as a coat, handbag, or program) across the heads of the people sitting in those seats.

When you pass in front of someone say, "Excuse me please," not "'scuse" or "Pardon." If someone has to stand up to let you through say, "Thank you."

If you have to pass in front of someone a second time, say, "I'm sorry to disturb you again" and "thank you" as you go by.

If you are seated and someone passes in front of you, hold your knees sideways to give that person as much room as you can. If this is impossible, then stand (even half-way) and quickly be seated. Respond with a courteous, "Certainly" or "Surely" when someone excuses herself to pass in front of you.

Once seated, get yourself situated quickly. Remove your coat and place it on the back of your seat. If you're wearing a hat, take it off immediately. It's better to do so on your own than be asked to remove it.

Keep your feet out of the aisles and passageways.

Audience Taboos

- Talking during a performance

  Don't; you must be perfectly silent! A concert involves listening skills more than visual concentration, so don't distract those around you. If you've already seen the play, keep the plot to yourself.

- Humming, singing, toe or finger tapping

  The performers don't need any help. A great foot exercise, however, is tapping your toes inside your shoes!

- Taking your shoes off

  Keep your shoes on your feet. Someone I know once took his shoe off in the theater and it rolled underneath the next four rows of seats. How embarrassing to retrieve it.

- Eating

  Candy and other foods shouldn't be passed or eaten during a performance. Even the rattling of candy papers can disturb others. (Opening wrappers slowly just prolongs the torture.) If you think you'll need a cough drop, have it unwrapped and ready to pop in your mouth.

- Reading

  Look through your program before the performance begins. What you don't know when the curtain goes up will have to wait until it's down again.

- Lights or photographs

    Equally annoying are those people who use small flashlights or take photographs. In some cases, flashing can be temporarily blinding to the performers, but cameras aren't usually permitted anyway.

- Sleeping, groaning, or sighing with boredom

    Sleeping is the least of these evils—as long as you don't snore!

- Booing, hissing, whistling, and laughing

    The performers can and *do* hear the audience. Put yourself in their position, so zip it up.

- Gum chewing

    With gum chewing come cracking and other noises, which are totally inexcusable. Do not chew gum in the theater (or anyplace else).

- Program rustling

    This indicates that you aren't listening, and you should be!

- Jingling bracelets, loud ticking or beeping watches and beepers

    Wear these items to sporting events, where the distractions will not be heard, instead of to concerts or the theater.

- Opening and closing purses, opera glasses, or binocular cases

    Do this before, not during, the performance.

- Leaving early

    Wait until the entire performance is over before you put on your coat, hat, and gloves.

Abide by these tips, and believe it or not, you'll enjoy going to the theater!

Performers love which of the following?
- ❏ *rustling*
- ❏ *snoring*
- ❏ *your attention*
- ❏ *beepers*
- ❏ *flash bulbs*
- ❏ *applause*

Applause

Applauding is your way to say thank you. There are certain times when you applaud:

- **Theater**   At the end of each act
- **Ballet**   When each musical or dance selection is finished
- **Concert**   When the conductor walks on the stage and faces the audience or when he turns to the audience to take his bow, indicating that the selection is over
- **Opera**   After the arias, at each curtain call

If in doubt about when to applaud let someone else start. A woman applauds by holding her left hand still, palm up, and gently taps it with the fingers of her right hand.

Intermission

You may proceed to the lobby during intermission. This is the time to have something to eat or drink. You may leave your coat on your chair, but take your purse with you.

The signal to return to your seats, which might be dimming of the lights, bells ringing, or a verbal announcement, is usually given two minutes before the performance resumes. When the signal is given, return to your seat rather than continue talking, drinking, or people-watching. It's very annoying to the audience and the performers when you come in after the second act has begun.

Attire

Wear your "good" clothes to the theater. A party dress or a blazer is fine, especially if you have something special to do before or after the theater.

On the whole, most people who attend the theater are well-behaved, attentive, and quiet. They're interested in the performance or they wouldn't be there — just like you, right?

raveling

Up and Away!

Traveling on a plane is fast and fun—and packed with opportunities to use your good manners.

Wear nice clothes (that means no tank tops, short shorts, or ripped jeans), and if you take your shoes off during flight, make sure you have on socks.

When you pass through the security gate, never, ever, ever make jokes or statements about hijacking or bombs. It's humorless.

If you're traveling alone, hand the airline employee your ticket and boarding pass, and then as you enter the airplane, the flight attendant will look at your boarding pass and show you where to sit. All seats are clearly marked. You may be in the first class section, where the seating is roomier, the meals are more elaborate, the service is generally better, and the cocktails (not yet for you) are free. And, oh yes, the tickets are pricier. Or, you may be in the coach section, where there is enough room, the meals and service are fine, and the tickets are less expensive.

Wherever you're seated, quickly get yourself situated and comfortable. If you have a coat or a carry-on bag, ask the flight attendant to place it in the overhead compartment for you. Get out the tapes or magazines or whatever else you want to keep at your seat, before you board so that 150 people don't have to stand there waiting for you to scurry through your bag, before placing it in the overhead compartment.

You'll see lighted signs reminding you to fasten your seat belts. Obey them. Before takeoff, the flight attendant will go over some safety precautions. You may already be familiar with these, but the person next to you might not.

Once you're airborne, you may be served a meal, a snack, or just a beverage. Pay attention to what the flight attendant offers you to drink so you don't have to ask to have the list repeated four times. Avoid pushing the call button every ten minutes. Don't ask for a refill or a second helping unless you're offered one.

28

Your tray unlatches from the seat in front of you to become your personal dining table. (Table manners are the same in the air!) If something should accidentally spill, the flight attendant will help you, so don't hesitate to ask. Refer to the flight attendant as "flight attendant," not "Hey You."

If the person next to you starts a conversation with you, and you feel like talking, fine. If not, don't be rude, simply answer the question and go on reading your book, looking out the window, or whatever. Don't strike up a conversation with a stranger.

Once you're seated, stay put. Sprinting up and down the aisle, won't help a long flight, but an occasional walk to stretch out is OK.

Use the restroom before you board. An airplane is one of the few places where men and women share the same lavatory facilities. Sometimes the wait can be long. Be patient and when it's finally your turn be as quick as possible. This is not the time to braid your hair. Make sure your visit to the lavatory is an absolute necessity. Place the towels in the proper disposal bin — not on the floor, on the sink or in the toilet.

You'll be a real annoyance to other passengers if you:

- ☛ Drop your seat back suddenly. You may recline, but be considerate of the person behind you. (You don't want to catch them mid-drink.)
- ☛ Slam the tray into its latch, jarring the person in front of you.
- ☛ Toe-tap or kick the seat in front of you (really jarring her).
- ☛ Clickety clank on your laptop.

If you feel queasy, call the flight attendant. If you're suddenly going to be physically sick, use the bag in the seat pocket in front of you.

If you're on an all-night flight, ask for a blanket and a pillow if you're sleepy. Once the lights have been dimmed, be especially quiet because others are trying to sleep. If you're not tired, you may want to watch the movie (if there is one) or keep your overhead light on to read.

As the plane begins to descend, you'll see the "Fasten Seat Belts" sign light up again. Finally, you're on the ground (at last) don't rush to the door. Gather all of your personal belongings, wait your turn, then step out into the aisle. A backpack attack can cause serious injury to the person receiving the blow. Be careful.

As you deplane, say "thank you" and "goodbye" to the airline personnel standing at the door. Never tip an airline attendant.

Once you've reached the terminal, wait at the gate for whomever is to meet you. Don't wander through the airport alone.

Traveling by Train

Train travel can be a lot of fun, especially if an entire group is going somewhere. Seating is generally open, which means that you may sit anywhere. There is a dining car and sometimes a cocktail lounge or sleeping cars on the train. Keep your ticket with you because the conductor can ask to see it at anytime. Lavatories are usually located at the end of each car. Sit back and enjoy the scenery.

Automobile

Traveling by car can be either a real drag or a fun experience with lots of learning opportunities. Play games, sing songs, read, needlepoint, or listen to music during long car rides. Don't ask whomever is driving to constantly stop for you to go to the bathroom or get something to eat—you'll never arrive at your destination if you keep stopping. And don't ask, "Are we almost there?" or "How much longer?" if you've only been driving for 10 minutes.

Carpooling

Be ready and waiting for your driver whether going to school or being picked up after school. Greet whoever's driving, and anyone else in the car. Don't sit on or deliberately try to squash anyone. Hold onto your books. Don't even think about exercising your vocal chords. Don't bang or slam the car door. As you get out, a friendly "Thank you" is most appreciated. If you think riding in a carpool is bad, try driving carpool.

Buses and Subways

If you are taking a public bus, have your money or pass ready when you step onto the bus. Find a seat and sit quietly until it's time to get off. Don't eat or drink.

If you're on a tour bus or going someplace with your class or a group, thank the bus driver when you leave. He has probably been listening to your singing, gabbing, and giggling for quite awhile. He deserves a smile.

Sandwiched on the subway? The rules are pretty basic. Don't block the doors, hold onto the handrail, offer an older person your seat, let passengers enter before you get off.

Your Destination

You might think that when you're in another city, state, or country, you don't have to be your usual, well-behaved self. Guess again!

Just because you may not know anyone, you should still be kind and courteous and avoid doing anything that would be rude.

How do your rate these travel behaviors?

Rushing to the door
❏ *go for it* ❏ *no way*

"Are we there yet?"
❏ *go for it* ❏ *no way*

Slamming car doors
❏ *go for it* ❏ *no way*

Thanking the driver
❏ *go for it* ❏ *no way*

Eating on public transit
❏ *go for it* ❏ *no way*

Kicking seat in front
❏ *go for it* ❏ *no way*

Take Me Out to The Ball Game

When you're at a sporting event, respect the players and the surroundings. That means no unsportsmanlike behavior such as yelling obscenities or throwing things (cups, wrappers, peanuts, or shoes) on the playing surface. You (as well as those around you) should enjoy the game! For all sports, spectator behavior is the same.

- Consider the event and dress appropriately. It can be chilly in a large stadium or arena, or it may be scorching hot in an open stadium. You'll enjoy the event more if you aren't freezing or sweating the whole time.

- Sporting events are informal and casual, but pants (jeans are OK), skirts, or walking shorts (never short-shorts) should be worn. Never wear old, ragged T-shirts or ripped jeans. You should dress nicely, but comfortably.

- Arrive on time.

- Let the usher help you find your seats.

- Stand for the National Anthem and either participate or *be silent.*

- If you must take your transistor radio to a sporting event, please use earplugs.

- When you want to get up during a game, wait for a lull in the action or a break in the play.

- Cheer and get excited—especially when your team scores. Remember that those sitting behind you can't see when you jump up with every play, but be considerate and come back down.

- Chanting at school games is fun, but it's inappropriate to call names or boo the officials or other team for any reason.

- Don't seat-hop. Maybe your seats aren't as good as the ones in the front row, but they are your seats. Besides, think of how embarrassing it would be if someone arrives late only to find *you* in his seat.

- At sporting events, unlike the theater, you may eat and drink at your seat and even discard your peanut shells, wrappers, and cups on the floor. However, no one appreciates walking out with wet or sticky shoes or peanut shells in her hair so don't be sloppy.

- Keep your feet off the seat back in front of you even if no one is sitting in it.

- When you are someone's guest at a sporting event, eat dinner or lunch at home before you leave. Don't wait until you get to the game to chow down on hot dogs, pretzels, and whatever else they're buying. Wait until you're offered something to eat or drink; don't ask.

- If you don't like a certain sport and are bored to death, sorry; and it's impolite to sit and talk nonstop with your neighbor.

- Brush up on the sport, if you know nothing about it, before you attend a game or match. At least you'll have an idea of what's happening.

1, 2, 3 Strikes... You're Out!

It's not whether you win or lose, but how you play the game that's important. This old saying is true, though it's always more fun to win. When you're playing a sport, keep these things in mind:

- Arrive on time, whether it's to practice or a game.

- Leave all of your jewelry at home while you're playing, and keep your hair off your face. You're not in a beauty contest, you're playing a sport. And make sure your shoes are tied before you take to the field or court.

- Have your own clubs, tennis or golf balls, racquet, stick, glove, or whatever else you need. Don't mooch off your teammates or opponents.

- Respect for your coach, who may be someone's parent donating valuable time. He or she has a big job trying to keep the entire team (and their parents) happy. It takes a special person to coach young people.

- If the coach doesn't put you in as much as your teammates, don't pout or break into tears on the bench. Not everyone can be tops in everything—maybe you're better at math, art, singing or dancing, or just being yourself.

- Thank your coach after every game and practice. Make a special effort to do this; it will mean so much to her.

- On a given day, any player or team can win or lose! If you can't lose graciously, don't play the game.

- Games are based on rules. Know and accept the rules of all the sports you play. The object is to make it fair for each side. A poor sport complains about rules, referees, plays, coaches, and everything else. A complainer is no fun.

Is this sportsman-like behavior? Hint: only one is allowed:
- ❑ *cutting in line*
- ❑ *arriving late*
- ❑ *boo-ing at officials*
- ❑ *seat-hopping*
- ❑ *talking non-stop*
- ❑ *leaving your peanut shells on the floor*

- Avoid arguments. Instead, state that you thought the ball was "in" on the serve. Your opponent will know what you mean. You still won't gain the point, but you'll have peace of mind and remain a good sport!

- Don't use obscenities or berate the other team, especially if you lost. This is poor sportsmanship.

- A confident person attributes a victory to the entire team and a conceited person takes all of the credit himself. A team sport is a team effort, be it a team win or a team loss.

- Be eager to shake hands with the other team after the game. Always say "Nice game" or "Great game." Say something complimentary no matter who won or lost. Slapping the opponents' hands hard, spitting in your hand first, or throwing your tennis racquet destroys the game for everyone.

- Compliment your opponent on her good play or console her on her bad luck (not her bad playing). Let your own failures go unsaid.

- Improve your own shortcomings; admire ability in others. Be a gracious, cheerful loser and be a quiet, humble winner—no need to show off. You are confident enough with yourself.

- It's OK to be humble, but don't tell a not-so-great player that you're terrible just to turn around and beat him into the ground.

- Don't complain of a sore toe or headache or pulled muscle after you've lost, and never feel one coming on when it looks like you're going to lose (unless it's the truth).

- If you make a bet with someone, be prepared to pay up if you lose. There is no excuse for cheating with anything concerning sports.

- If you use a locker room at your or another school, leave it clean. Put the towels where they belong. Throw your trash away, don't leave it on the floor. Don't write on the walls or mirrors, and take all of your belongings with you.

- Don't leave your wet or dirty uniform in your bag until the stink is overpowering. Take it out right when you get home; whoever does the laundry at your house will appreciate this courtesy.

- At the conclusion of the game, walk with the crowd, not through the crowd. Don't shove. If your parents are picking you up, be at your meeting spot on time; don't lollygag and relive the game.

Winning and losing are part of everything you'll do in life. If you're a poor sport in games, you'll be a poor sport in life. Sportsmanship, like courage, is merely grace under pressure. If you're losing, try harder. It takes a real "winner" to be a good loser.

Museums and Libraries

Museums

- In order for the exhibits to be enjoyed by everyone, as they really should be, you must be courteous and patient while waiting in line when visiting a museum.
- Don't walk in front of others viewing the exhibits. Speak softly. If someone is standing in your way, be patient until they move on.
- Don't eat, drink or touch anything in a museum.
- If you are on a guided tour, feel free to ask questions.
- However, don't make comments or begin conversations with strangers.
- When visiting an art museum show respect for the art (even if you don't like it) and the rights of those who are there to enjoy it.

Library

- If you're in a library, whether public or at school, this is not the place to socialize.
- Speak softly. Ask for help in locating a book, if you need it. Avoid loud laughter.
- Don't "dog ear," tear or write on any of the pages. If you don't want a book, put it right back where you found it.
- Don't leave it on the table.
- Check out the books you've decided on. Return your books on time and to the right location.
- A library can be a great place to study. Take advantage of the quietness.

Public Appearances

Picnics in the Park

Remember to clean up your mess and dispose of your trash in the containers provided, not on the ground. Avoid hanging around and playing in the water fountain. Should a sign say "no fishing" or "no swimming", "no rollerblading" that's exactly what it means.

Bicycling, Rollerblading and Skateboarding

Take a few lessons, if you don't know how to start, turn, cruise and *most importantly,* STOP. It really isn't polite to barrel into others.

If you're wheeling on a sidewalk or park path, stay to the right and don't sway from side to side. The *entire* width of the path does not belong to you. Say, "on your left" when you decide to pass someone.

You know to wear a helmet and other protective guards on body parts you want to keep in tact.

Running, Jogging, Walking

If you're running in the park, keep up the pace, don't slow down those behind you. Don't run three to four abreast. As you pass someone, smile and say "hi", but don't stop and start a conversation. Runners don't want to cool down and talk.

Amusement Parks

OBEY all ride rules. Don't run, push or shove to get to a certain car or seat. Fasten everything that should be fastened in order to keep you safely inside the car. All this is for your protection. Don't stand, rock the car or throw things out.

Scared on a ride? S-C-R-E-A-M to release your anxiety. Don't force, chide or make fun of someone who is not as daring as you.

Whether you have saved your money to spend on your school picnic or have been given a certain amount, stick to your limit and don't borrow from your friends.

Set a specific time and place where your parents can find you periodically. Be there on time.

Swimming

You will not make a splash if you do just that! Avoid splashing sunbathers. Some people don't like being splashed or dunked even though they're in the water.

Another thing to avoid while swimming is to constantly ask someone to "watch" you do something.

Don't ask friends to watch your things. It is inconsiderate to tie them down while you're off playing.

If your friend does not swim as well as you — so what? Have fun anyway. Nothing is more frightening than being afraid of the water, so don't jeer or make fun of someone who does not swim. This means no dunking.

If you are lucky enough to be at the beach, don't kick or throw sand on anyone who is sunbathing or minding her own business. Don't destroy someone's sandcastle.

When you are invited to swim, you must be responsible for your own towel and suntan lotion. Don't expect to have towels furnished when you go to someone's home.

Towels provided you at a hotel or club are not to be removed from the premises.

Waiting in Line

Most of the time waiting in a long line is *no fun*. However, it is fair and pushing, shoving and trying to sneak ahead won't help one bit.

Mall Manners

Yelling, running, and being obnoxious are all taboo. If a store sign states NO eating or drinking, that's what it means. Avoid using store windows for combing your hair or looking at yourself.

Video Store

Pass behind people who are looking at the display shelves, not in front. Avoid gathering up 15 new releases to only put 14 back 20 minutes later. Put the videos back where you found them. It's unfair to hold up the checkout line while you search through your wallet for your card. Have it and your money ready when you check out. If someone is checking out a film you've already seen, keep your comments to yourself. No one is interested in hearing your critique of the plot.

Escalators

Stay on one step only, do not run up and down on the escalators or try to go up backwards. If the escalator is broken, don't use it.

People Walker

If you are standing still, stay to the right and keep walking if you're on the left. Don't run or try to race your friend who is walking alongside.

Doors

Whoever gets to the door first opens it. When someone opens the door for you, respond with a smile and "thank you." A revolving door is not a merry-go-round. Only one person in a cubicle at one time.

Elevators

In an elevator, stand quietly. If you see someone running for the elevator, please push the *door open* button. Do not push any of the buttons as you get off. Let anyone getting off the elevator get out before you get in.

Shopping

Your Favorite Pastime

- You thought shopping was your total getaway from manners - wrong! Shopping is fun, or can be more fun if you are shopping and making purchases for yourself. How selfish, but true. Shop with only two friends at a time. More than two usually causes total confusion and chaos.

- Always ask a salesperson if you may try something on. Then, be gentle with the clothing you try on.

- Put the clothing back on the hangers when you are finished. Do not leave the dressing room a total disaster.

- Keep from peeking underneath your dressing room into another one (even if your friend is in the other one).

- Take all of your belongings, but none of the store's when you leave the dressing room.

- Many times a sales person has had a bad morning or day and your being grouchy only makes the situation worse. If the department does not have something you want, it is not the fault of the sales person, so why should she be the object of your anger? She shouldn't.

- Wait your turn, when you see a salesperson is busy.

- Avoid shouting across the counter or interrupting to ask where something might be.

- When a salesperson says, "May I help you?" You may reply with, "No thank you. I am just looking." or, "Yes, thank you, I am looking for..."

- Snide remarks are unnecessary. Keep the sales receipt in case you must return an item. Say, "thank you" to the salesperson after you have made a purchase.

- Avoid running or shouting through any store for any reason.

- Toys are not to be tested while in the store. Do not pick up anything breakable.

- Avoid eating or drinking in stores.

Members Only

Private clubs, such as country or athletic clubs, are for people who pay an initiation fee to become a member and then a monthly fee just to belong! Many of them are pretty snazzy.

When you're at a country club, you'll notice that there's no money exchanged. Everything is charged to the member's bill, which he pays at a later time.

You should dress nicely when you attend a club. There are only certain areas where you may wear your swimming suit; never walk around in your bare feet. A dress or skirt, for ladies and nice pants, a collared shirt, or a sportcoat, for gentlemen should be worn to dinner. Follow the lead of your host or hostess, if you're not sure of the proper thing to do at a club.

In the rest rooms, just like in an elaborate restaurant, there might be a person who will hand you a towel or offer you some hand cream. Need a band aid, safety pin or a spritz of hairspray? The attendant is the person to ask. There will be a little dish on the counter with some change already in it. You may tip the attendant 50 cents even if your hostess already has. And, "Thank you" is always appropriate.

Don't wander around the club without your parents or host or hostess.

How do I dress at a club?
❑ *swimsuit*
❑ *jacket or skirt*
❑ *as hostess does?*
❑ *old t-shirt*

Keep your feet off of couches or chairs and don't lean on the walls. Make sure to put your glass on a coaster, not on an unprotected surface (this is good anywhere). Behave as a guest in a private club the same way you would as a guest in someone's home. Good manners in clubs are the same as good manners elsewhere. A gracious guest always gets another invitation.

CHAPTER THREE

Parties, Parties and More

ostess With the Mostest

A party is one way of bringing together a special group of people at one time, whether it's a small gathering of a few close friends, or a huge celebration. A party should be fun.

Planning your party is half the excitement of having it. Discuss the important details such as date, time, number of guests, kind of party, what you will serve and where it will be with your parents first.

Guest List

If your guest list must be limited, start with your favorites. It's nice to have a variety of friends, however, you may wish to invite just a certain group from school.

Don't discuss the party around anyone who is not invited. This can cause hurt feelings.

Invitations

You may purchase, design your own or call your guests to invite them. No erasures or smudges on the written invitations. A written invitation answers these questions:

- **Who**   hostess's name
- **Where**   address and a map
- **What**   kind of party; skating, sleepover, dinner, outdoors
- **When**   day, date and time)
- **Why**   special event or occasion; birthday, going away
- **RSVP**   a French phrase, "Repondez s'il vous plait" which translated means, *respond if you please.* Avoid the phrase "regrets only."

Mail your invitations about seven to ten days prior to the party. Don't forget your return address on the back of the envelope.

Keep your invitation list next to the telephone so that when your guests call to reply you can check off their names.

Invitation

- Occasion: _____
- Time: _____
- Place: _____
- Date: _____
- Dress/Theme: _____
- RSVP: _____

Decorations

If you are focusing on a theme - great. Use balloons, crepe paper, banners and whatever else you can come up with for a festive occasion.

The Serving Table

Set a pretty table for a party or tea. Maybe you're using your mother's good china and silver. (Lucky you.)

If your party is a pool party, scavenger hunt, barbecue where everything is outside, then by all means use paper plates, napkins, cups, and plastic utensils.

In other words, if your party is casual, everything about it should all be casual. If it is more elegant, then everything should be equally elegant.

Your place mats or tablecloth should match or coordinate with your napkins. A tablecloth belongs on a serving table. When you set the serving table, place the napkins first, followed by plates and utensils. Then the "goodies", whatever they may be. Place the punch cups or glasses next to the punch bowl or drinks you're serving.

Food looks so much more appealing if a paper doily is on the tray first. Sometimes the doilies come in colors, but you'll always be safe with white.

Fresh flowers add a nice touch to any party and should be on the serving table.

Here is a "Party Planner" you can use ▶

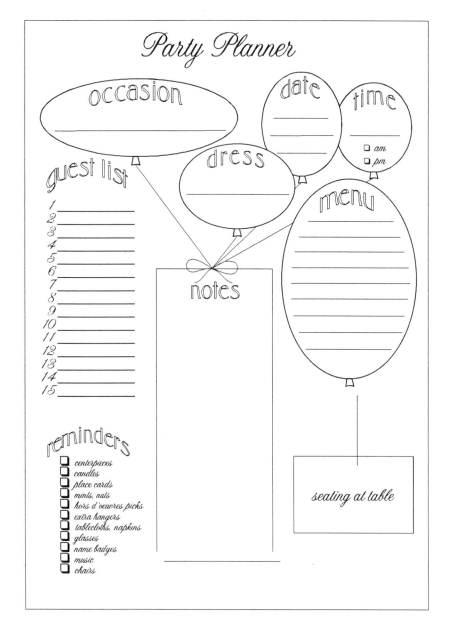

Party Planner

occasion

date

time

☐ am
☐ pm

guest list

dress

menu

1
2
3
4
5
6
7
8
9
10
11
12
13
14
15

notes

reminders

☐ centerpieces
☐ candles
☐ place cards
☐ mints, nuts
☐ hors d'oeuvres picks
☐ extra hangers
☐ tablecloths, napkins
☐ glasses
☐ name badges
☐ music
☐ chairs

seating at table

After all the preparation and planning, it's time to party! The party begins with the arrival of the first guest.

Be ready. Greet each guest at the door. Take her coat or show her where to put it. Introduce her to your parents and all adults at the party. Then introduce your guests as they arrive to the others.

May I Get You Some Punch?

A hostess gets each guest the first drink. You may then suggest that each person helps himself. Or, if you have an extra sister or neighbor, who would like to help you, she can be in charge of pouring punch.

Pouring Punch

Pick up a punch cup with your *left* hand, handle facing away from. Hold the cup over the punch bowl and fill the cup only two-thirds full, never to the very rim of the cup. (See photo at right, top. ▶)

Place the ladle back in the punch bowl. With the filled cup still in your left hand, pick up a napkin with your right hand and place it under the punch cup. Now hand both to your guest. Since the handle is still facing "away" from you, your guest can accept it by the handle. (See photo at right, bottom. ▶)

A Good Time

As the hostess, your only concern is that your guests are having a good time. If someone is shy and all alone, introduce him to a more outgoing guest. If someone should break or spill something, be gracious. Clean it up. Then say, "Don't worry; those things happen."

It is okay for the hostess to participate in games, but she never takes a prize.

The Party's Over

When the party is over, walk each guest to the door and thank them for coming. Don't yell from another area.

Don't invite any guest to "stay longer." Thank your parents for a super party and then help clean up as all good hostesses do.

Overnight

If your friend is spending the night, make sure your room is neat and clean. Put out a clean towel, washcloth, drinking cup and fresh bar of soap. Check to see if he needs toothpaste and no doubt your mother has new toothbrushes to spare just in case.

Allow your guest to use the bathroom "first" before going to bed.

When your mother says, "lights out" this is exactly what she means. Be considerate of others in the house. Keep the television low and don't yell, laugh loud, or turn up music so that no one can sleep.

On Any Occasion

Make your guest feel welcome and at home. Avoid reading a letter or talking on the telephone in front of your guest. Give your friend a choice of games to play or which television programs to watch.

If more than one friend comes over, be careful not to exclude anyone.

Always serve your guests first. Don't eat or drink in front of them.

Don't invite a friend to stay any longer than the originally scheduled plan, unless you discuss it first and in private, with your mother.

To the pushy friend who invites himself, you might say, "I'm sorry, but I cannot have you over tomorrow. Maybe another time. I'll call you."

If your guest is from out of town, it is nice to plan some special activities that include seeing your town. Or a little party to meet some of your friends or classmates.

Guest With the Best

Have you ever wondered why you were invited to a lot of parties? You are popular, well liked *and* a gracious guest. You know how to behave at another person's home.

Accept With Pleasure

When you see the letters RSVP on an invitation, you should reply as quickly as possible. RSVP stands for a French phrase, "Repondez s'il vous plait" which translated means "Respond, if you please."

If "Regrets Only" is on your invitation, then respond only if you cannot attend.

Tell your hostess you're looking forward to her party:

- ☛ "I can come to your party and am really looking forward to it."

If you cannot attend, simply say,

- ☛ "I am sorry but I cannot come to your party. Thank you for thinking of me."

If you decline an invitation, you may not accept an invitation from someone else, especially if it's for something you would rather do.

Dress Accordingly.

Ask the hostess, if in doubt.

Greetings

Arrive on the button.

Say hello to the host's mother and all adults at the party. A pleasant smile and friendly, "Hi, how are you" to the guests. Go up and introduce yourself to anyone you don't know. Include the loner in your conversation.

Yes, I'll Have Some Punch

As the guest, accept the punch by the handle. The napkin stays in your hand, it is not lifted to your mouth with the cup. Avoid hanging out at the punch bowl too long.

When being served anything from a tray such as cookies or candy, the one you touch is the one you take. And, you always take the one closest to you. Do not poke your (or anyone else's) finger in several pieces of candy to see which one you prefer. Or plunder through a tray of cookies for the right one?

Anything being served in a frill (the paper the candy or petit four is in), is picked up "frill and all." The empty frill is placed on your plate when you are finished, or ask where to put it.

When you have a plate, you may take two of whatever is being served. If you don't have a plate, ONLY one.

A small spoon in a bowl of nuts or mints is to be used. Take a few in the spoon and put them in your left hand. Put the spoon back in the bowl and then eat the morsels with your right hand. Just a few in the spoon at a time. You are not digging to see how many nuts you can balance on the spoon.

Don't put a cup or plate on an unprotected table unless told to do so by the hostess. If you don't know where to put something, ask the hostess.

Having Fun

Participate fully in the games or activities the hostess has planned for you, even if you don't want to. Somebody wins; somebody loses. Don't be upset and pout if you don't win. Do have a good time. Everyone loves to invite someone who has fun.

Avoid being "life of the party" and trying to take over, even if you are bored.

Oops!

Don't make a scene if you accidentally spill or drop something. Say how sorry you are, then help clean it up. If it's something your parents have to replace, do it as soon as possible.

Time to Leave

You don't take a "doggie bag" home from a party. Don't stuff your purse with any of the refreshments. What you don't eat at the party stays there.

Leave at the stated on the invitation. If the hostess invites you to stay longer, don't.

Don't forget to say, "goodbye and thank you" to all the adults and then to your friend. Adding, of course, that you had a great time.

A telephone call the next day to thank the hostess is a nice gesture. A thank you note is especially gracious. These courtesies will get you more invitations.

Overnight

A little gift for the hostess is always nice and thoughtful. Maybe some fresh flowers, a box of candy or some homemade cookies. Something the whole family can enjoy.

When someone tells you to make yourself at home they don't mean for you to leave your shoes, hairbrush and pajama's all over the house. Put your belongings only where the hostess tells you. Keep all of your things together

Tuck some lifesavers or a bag of peanuts in your suitcase for an emergency hunger attack.

Leave the bathroom in the same neat, clean order in which you found it. This is especially important if your friend shares a bathroom with the rest of her family. Ask where to put the wet washcloth and towel.

Greet all members of the household whenever you see them. If you have nothing to say at least smile. Don't ignore anyone.

Make your bed, or pick up your sleeping bag. Take the sheets off the bed before you leave.

Write a thank you note as soon as you get home or call the next day.

Which of the following are guest "do's"?
- ❏ *greet family*
- ❏ *stay longer*
- ❏ *repeat gossip*
- ❏ *thank the hostess*
- ❏ *be tidy*
- ❏ *open drawers*

On Any Occasion

☛ Always say hello to your friend's parents.

☛ Don't open drawers, closets or become a spy. When a door is closed, knock first. Don't read anyone's mail.

☛ Don't answer the telephone at someone else's house, unless asked to do so. Ask permission if you need to use the telephone and make your call brief.

☛ Don't ask personal questions or become involved in a family's personal conversation. Whatever you hear at someone's home STAYS there. You repeat nothing to anyone.

- If asked which games you would like to play or television programs you would like to watch, state your choice.

- It is also very gracious to tell the hostess you would like her to choose. Don't get into the "I don't care" routine.

- If you have been invited to stay for lunch or dinner, don't accept until you call your mother. If your mother says "no" then say, "I am sorry, but my mother says I cannot stay this time. Thank you anyway."

- If offered something to eat or drink, by all means accept if you want it, but don't ask for cookies, candy, soda or anything else.

- If you are so thirsty or so hungry you're going to pass out, then you may ask for a drink of water or a cracker or get out those lifesavers you brought.

CHAPTER FOUR

Dining

Setting the Scene

You have probably been setting the table for a long time, but has it been the proper way? Practice setting the table every chance you get.

In case you forget what goes where just remember that F-O-R-K and L-E-F-T have four letters. K-N-I-F-E, S-P-O-O-N and R-I-G-H-T have five letters. ▶

Your forks go on the left and your spoons and knives go on the right. Never again should you forget!

The Properly Set Table

DINNER PLATE	Center of place setting
DINNER FORK	Left of dinner plate
SALAD FORK	Left of dinner fork
SEAFOOD FORK	Left of salad fork or on right next to soup spoon
DINNER KNIFE	Right of dinner plate, blade faces in
TEASPOON	Right of knife
SOUP SPOON	Right of knife
SALAD PLATE	Left of forks
BREAD/BUTTER PLATE	Left, above forks
BUTTER KNIFE	Placed horizontally on bread/butter plate
DESSERT FORK/SPOON	Horizontally above dinner plate
	Fork handle to left; spoon handle to right
WATER GLASS	Above dinner plate to the right
WINE GLASS	Right of water glass
CUP AND SAUCER	Above soup spoon
NAPKIN	Left of forks, traditionally

L E F T
▼ ▼ ▼ ▼
F O R K

R I G H T
▼ ▼ ▼ ▼ ▼
S P O O N
K N I F E

Tools of the Trade

All utensils do not have to be placed on the table at once. They may be brought to the table with their course. Silverware is generally placed in its order of use. When if doubt, follow the following rule:

- ☞ Begin at the outside and work toward the center.

Napkin: Traditionally, your napkin is folded and placed to the left of the forks. Wait to see if the host is going to say grace, then unfold your napkin only half way and place it on your lap. In a restaurant, you place it on your lap immediately upon being seated. Sometimes the waiter will do it for you.

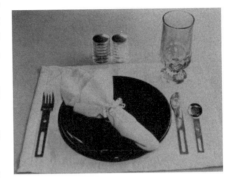

The days of tucking your napkin into your waist or tying it around your neck are *over* except for lobster and sometimes pasta.

Use your napkin to "BLOT" your lips. Do not rub. Always blot before taking a drink. **Never** use your napkin to wipe or blow your nose.

If you have to excuse yourself during dinner, crumple your napkin and place it to the left of your plate (not on the chair).

At the end of dinner, again crumple it and place it to the left or right of your plate. Don't fold it back into its original folds. Don't leave it in the center of your plate or on the floor.

Service Plate: This is the plate seen under an appetizer, soup bowl, shrimp cocktail, ice cream even ice tea. Utensils are left on the service plate rather than the cup or bowl. A large service plate, which is called a charger is removed when the entree is served.

Dinner Plate: This large plate is for the entree or main course.

Dinner Fork: The large fork next to the plate. Use for entree. Cut anything you can with a fork.

Salad Plate: Smaller than your dinner plate. Salad may be served as a separate course or eaten with your entree.

Salad Fork: Smaller than the dinner fork. Use for salad, *only* if salad is a separate course.

Seafood Fork: This is the tiny fork with only three tines. It is to the left of the forks on the outside or to the right of your soup spoon

Bread and Butter Plate: Smaller than the salad plate. Use for rolls, breads, jams, jellies and butter.

Bread and Butter Knife: A small knife that is not used for cutting, but to spread butter on breads and corn on the cob.

Soup Spoon: This is the large spoon to the outside right and it means soup is coming. When finished with your soup, leave the spoon on the service plate. If there is no service plate, leave the spoon in the bowl.

Teaspoon: A small spoon that is used for dessert, coffee, tea, hot chocolate, but not soup. Place this spoon on the saucer or service plate when finished.

Dinner Knife: The large knife next to the dinner plate. The blade faces the plate. Use for cutting meat and anything that cannot be cut with a fork. Do not lick your knife, balance peas on it or wave it in the air. Use it as a "pusher" to get food on your fork.

Water Glass: A water glass may be a tumbler (tall, straight) or a goblet, which means it has a stem. A tumbler is held by the base. One hand only. A stemmed glass by its stem.

Cup and Saucer: For coffee, tea, hot chocolate. The cup is held by its handle. May be brought to the table with dessert.

Zig Zag Method

In the United States, the preferred method of cutting meat is referred to as the "zig zag" method. Here is why.

Hold your fork in your left hand, handle in your palm and tines down in the piece of meat. The knife is in your right hand, handle in your palm. It is acceptable to cut up to three pieces of meat at one time. Then place your knife in its "rest" position across the top of your plate. Do not let your knife hang off your plate 'gang-plank' style. Transfer your fork to your right hand, tines up, and raise it to your mouth. Tines are up whenever your fork is in your right hand.

European Method

This is another method of cutting meat. This time your fork is kept in your left hand during the entire meal - no zig zagging. Tines are down when the fork is raised to your mouth. Knife may be held in your right hand, but not waved in the air.

Either method is OK. Both are acceptable in the United States and Europe. Concentrate when you practice and it will become smooth.

Finished Position

When you are finished with your entree, place your knife and fork next to each other diagonally across your plate.

Fork tines are up, knife blade facing left. Knife above the fork. This clue tells the waiter or hostess you are finished.

Bend your wrists slightly when cutting your meat and you will not elbow your neighbor.

Furthermore...

- Don't hold your utensils like a shovel or like weapons.
- To use your dessert utensils, secure food with fork and eat with spoon.
- Once you have put a utensil in your mouth, it is always placed on a plate, not on the table
- If the serving utensil is missing, ask for one, don't use yours.
- If you drop a utensil at someone's home pick it up if you can without putting your head in the next person's plate and ask for another one. In a restaurant, leave it and ask for another one.
- Are you still in doubt about which utensil to use? Follow the leader. Do as your hostess does. Otherwise use good common sense.
- Suppose you pick up the wrong utensil? So what... continue to use it and let your poise shine.

Practice at home so you won't have to put on good manners when you're out. Your knowledge of dining etiquette is a wonderful reflection on your upbringing.

Foreign Objects?

Place Cards: These are folded cards set at each person's place, on or above the dinner plate, with the guest's name on it. Be sure the names are easy to see. No, you may not move the place card if you don't like the person sitting next to you.

Napkin Ring: Remove the ring and place it above your dinner plate.

Saltcellar: A saltcellar is a tiny dish holding salt. Use the spoon that is with it. If there's no spoon, use the tip of your "clean" knife. If there are individual saltcellars you may use your fingers for a "pinch of salt."

Paper Wrappers: Wrappers should be tucked under the lip of your plate, unfolded. Butter and jam wrappers left on your butter plate.

Candles: It is not necessarily someone's birthday when candles are on the dinner table. Do not blow them out.. Only blow out the candles on your birthday cake, when it's your birthday.

Flowers: Fresh flowers add the finishing touch to a table setting. They should be low enough so that no one has a problem seeing anyone else.

Rules of etiquette are essentially the same whether it's a formal dinner with a lot of silverware, a holiday brunch with your family or a picnic with your friends. Good manners put everyone at ease.

Food Finesse

Oh, weren't you such a cute baby, sitting in your highchair, eating with your fingers, and dropping food on the floor? How adorable you were, laughing and talking with food in your mouth! Well, you still may be cute and adorable, but not because you eat like a baby.

Good manners take the struggle out of eating, whatever the situation. You'll be eating for the rest of your life, so be eager to try new foods. Here is a list of foods, some may be favorites, some you may not have tried before, that includes the proper way each should be eaten. (Remember, these are rules to be used as guidelines. When in doubt, rely on your common sense to get you through an unfamiliar situation.)

Butter: Butter is placed on your butter dish and then used to butter your bread. If you don't have a butter dish, put the butter on your dinner plate.

Bread, Rolls, Muffins, Biscuits: Break off a small portion; butter and eat only this much at a time. Don't butter or cut the whole roll. Break and butter your bread *over your butter plate* to keep the crumbs where they belong.

Celery, Olives, Radishes: Eaten with your fingers. The olive pit is removed from your mouth with your fingers.

Salad: Use your salad fork, if it is a separate course. Use your dinner fork if it is part of your entree. You may cut large pieces of lettuce with a knife.

Spaghetti: Wind a few strands at a time around a dinner fork.

Soup: Tilt the spoon *away* from you. You may also tilt the bowl away from you. If the soup is served in a cup with handles, pick it up and drink from it—just don't slurp.

Crackers: Sure, why not... put them in your soup, a few at a time. Large crackers should be eaten separately.

Corn on the Cob: Butter, salt, and eat a few rows at a time. Don't overdo it—butter drooling down your chin isn't a pretty sight.

Shrimp Cocktail: Use your seafood fork to dip into the cocktail sauce.

Cheese: Spread a little on a cracker; don't weigh it down.

Dips: Dip the munchie, raw veggie, chip, or cracker *only once, before* it enters your mouth. No double dipping!

Gravy or Sauce: Pour it on top of whatever it's meant for. Don't have everything on your plate drowning in gravy.

Jellies (Mint, Apple, Cranberry, etc.): Spoon them onto your plate next to the meat. Take a little on your fork and eat it with the meat.

French Fries: These are a finger food. Dip them into catsup; don't pour it all over your fries.

Baked Potato: Slit it with a knife, and push the ends toward the center with your fingers to open it. Add butter, sour cream, and other goodies, and eat the skin if you like.

Bacon: If crisp, it's a finger food.

Fried Chicken: It's generally a finger food, but follow your host or hostess.

Barbecued Ribs: These are definitely a finger food.

Sandwiches: If large and messy, use a fork. If small, they're finger food.

Tacos: Hold it in your fingers and eat from one side only. When making your own taco, don't overfill it because one mouthful may be disastrous.

Pizza: Hold a piece in your fingers, curling up the sides to avoid losing the filling.

Hamburgers and Hot Dogs: Add your topping, but don't overdo it. Eat them with your fingers.

Strawberries: Large strawberries may be eaten whole. Grasp the stem and take a couple of bites. Leave the stem on your plate.

Grapes: Cut or break off a bunch, not one at a time.

Apples and Pears: Cut into quarters and core them. Then cut them into smaller pieces and eat with fork. In a casual situation, eat the pieces with fingers after halving and coring.

Melons (Cantaloupe, Honeydew, Casaba): Use a dessert spoon or a teaspoon.

Watermelon Wedges: Use a knife and fork. Place seeds on your plate with a cupped hand.

Bananas: At dinner, cut, peel, and eat with fork. On a picnic, peel and eat monkey style.

Cupcakes and Brownies: Break in half, then eat with your fingers.

Sticky Cake: Use your fork.

Pound Cake: Use your fingers to break and eat. If you add topping, use a fork or spoon.

Popsicles and Ice Cream Bars: Keep the paper on the bottom until you're finished.

And How Are You Served Your Food?

Food is served from the left; removed from the right. Drinks are served from the right. Bon appétit!

Restaurants

Almost everywhere you go you'll experience eating. It's the American way. There are brunches, lunches, teas, quick snacks, barbecues, picnics, banquets, buffets...and, of course, three regular meals a day.

If you practice your table manners at home every day, you will not have to put on "good manners" when you go someplace special. They'll be so natural you won't even have to think about what you're doing.

Going to a restaurant seems special. And, it is! Some restaurants are fancier than others; however, basic rules are the same.

◄ In a sophisticated restaurant there is a headwaiter or maitre d', who will greet you and seat you. He is easy to notice because he usually wears a tuxedo. By all means, check your coat because it's bulky to sit on during dinner.

Follow the headwaiter to the table. If there is no headwaiter, then the man leads. For now, it will probably be your dad, but later on it will be your date or escort.

Be sure to thank the headwaiter as he pulls out your chair and places your napkin on your lap. ▶

Any drink served with a tiny straw in it is to be used for stirring your drink. Don't drink from the straw.

Look over your menu and feel free to ask questions, if there is something you don't understand.

Answer all questions the waiter may ask such as how you like your meat cooked or what vegetable or salad dressing you would like. Your parents shouldn't have to speak for you.

Loud laughter and talk are impolite. Do not "table hop" or yell across the room to someone you see.

Don't keep getting up and whispering things to your mother or father.

In a restaurant you may ask for steak sauce, catsup or anything you might like that's not on the table.

It's always nice to thank the waiter when he serves you or refills your water glass.

Fast Food

When eating at a fast-food restaurant, your table manners are still the same.

If there is a long line, wait patiently. Know what you want to order before it's your turn. Have your money ready. Don't throw French fries to your friend at another table.

Don't blow the straw wrapper. Take it off and use the straw.

Stay seated; feet off booths, shirts and shoes ON.

Discard your papers, boxes and plastic utensils in the appropriate place.

Keep in mind that young children frequent fast food restaurants and they idolize cool teenagers, so mind your manners.

Table Manners

- Be neat and clean at the table, but don't groom yourself at the table.

- Come when called. Be on time!

- Find your place. At home, you probably have a regular place. At someone else's home, wait for the hostess to direct you or look for your place card. (No. You never switch place cards.)

- Wait for adults to be seated first.

- Once seated, display "good posture."

- Don't tip or tilt the chair backwards.

- Don't play with silverware, glassware, make nervous noises or pull on your finger joints. Heaven forbid you would even think of tapping the glass with a utensil.

- Hungry as you may be, WAIT for your hostess to begin or her direction for you to go start.

- If the host or hostess wishes to say grace before a meal, you may join in or bow your head quietly and respond with "Amen." This shows respect, even if it isn't your religion.

- Comments about what you dislike are not necessary.

- It is nice to compliment the hostess on something you especially like. However, lip smacking is not a compliment.

- Only two helpings of anything. No matter how much you like it.

- There is no excuse for chewing with your mouth open. This is very offensive to the person(s) eating with you.

- If you don't see it on the table, don't ask for it. Even if you put catsup on your pancakes, you will have to do without if it's not offered to you.

- Taste your food before putting salt or pepper on it.

- Say, "Please pass me the..." when you need something. Don't reach across anyone.

- Don't blow on a drink to cool it. Stir it quietly or just sit tight and wait for it to cool. If your food is too hot don't spit it out. In either case, take a drink of water.

- Don't dunk anything in your drink. This includes fingers and napkins.

- Blot your lips and swallow your food before taking a drink.

- Take small enough bites so that you can answer questions without putting up your index finger and pausing for a while.

- Don't talk with food in your mouth.

- Use a "pusher," your knife or a small piece of bread, if you have trouble picking something up. Not your fingers.

- NOTHING is finger licking good. When you eat finger foods, use your napkin, not your tongue to wipe your hands.

- If you accidentally "burp" excuse yourself. If you have to blow your nose, cough or sneeze, do it as quietly as possible and don't be embarrassed. It can't be helped. Don't make a scene or contribute to someone who is.

- Don't engage in gory conversation. Sit quietly and eat.

- Sayings such as, "I'm stuffed" or "I'm filled to the gills" are not necessary. Instead, put your utensils in their finished position and quietly wait to be excused.

- Don't brush away crumbs or stack your dishes when you are finished.

- A nice gesture is to offer to help clear the table, however, if the hostess says "no", don't insist. If she accepts your offer, be careful not to drop any of the dishes.

- If you find a bone, piece of gristle or any other foreign object in your mouth, remove it with your fingers and place it on your plate. Try to hide it under a piece of food.

- Always say, "No thank you" if offered a toothpick. Excuse yourself, go to the bathroom, and use dental floss if you need it.

- Spills. Offer to help clean up, but don't make a "big deal" out of it.

You won't be sent to jail for talking with food in your mouth or chewing with your mouth open, but you probably won't get a second invitation...

CHAPTER FIVE

Minding Your Manners

At Home

At Home, Where Manners Begin

There's no place like home to practice your manners. Let your family be the audience for your daily rehearsals. Your public performances will then be a real success. Everyday manners are the most important of all. When you spruce up and memorize a few rules of etiquette you fool some of the people some of the time. But when your courtesy is genuine, you don't have to worry about fooling anyone, anytime. Do your part to make your home the happiest place in the world.

Smile a lot at home. Let your family enjoy your real beauty.

Be generous with *please, thank you* and the toughest one, *I'm sorry.* Your family is important to you. Bet you could hardly live without them. So, treat them the same way you would your *best guest.*

First Things First

Whose fault is it that you might have gotten up on the wrong side of the bed? No one in your family! No need to take it out on them.

Greet all members of your family with a pleasant smile and "good morning." This can be real hard to do sometimes.

At dinner share with your family something that might have happened during the day. Ask your brothers, sisters, and parents how their days went. Get everyone's viewpoint on the news headlines. Solve a "world problem."

Don't be too eager to pick on a younger sibling, or pull rank. Name-calling, making fun of others or their efforts, is a no-no. Younger siblings think their teen sister or brother is cool, so don't disappoint them.

Keep family secrets just that. Don't tell anyone when personal or confidential matters are discussed within your family.

If someone calls you, do not yell, "WHAAAAT" or totally ignore the person. GET UP and see what they want. If you want something from someone, get up and go talk to the person. Don't yell.

No Trespassing, Private Property, Keep Out...

Wouldn't it be horrible to have to post such signs? Family members have a right to privacy, too. Which means DO NOT:

- ☛ Enter a room, without knocking first, if the door is closed.
- ☛ Open or read someone else's mail, even if there are no secrets between you and your sister.
- ☛ Snoop through anyone's drawers or closets.
- ☛ Listen in on anyone's telephone conversation.
- ☛ Borrow something without permission.
- ☛ Go into someone's purse or wallet.

More of What You've Already Heard...

Lend a hand at setting and clearing the table, loading the dishwasher, getting the mail, taking out the trash. Be careful because your mother "may" fall over if you do these things without being asked!!!

Only if you've been kidnapped should you leave a trail of your belongings. A trail at home for your mother to retrieve is unnecessary.

If you spill something, clean it up. If you drop something, pick it up. If *someone else* drops something, pick it up. Don't ignore, step on or over whatever is on the floor, pick it up, regardless of who dropped it. Get the message?

If you make a sandwich or some other concoction, clean up your mess.

Don't bang or slam doors, drawers or anything else for that matter.

Walk, don't run. Do not stomp up and down stairs like an elephant

The volume on your CD player is for *your* listening pleasure, not that of your neighbor's.

Walls stand alone, and so should you. Don't lean on the walls or sit on the arms or backs of chairs and couches. Keep your feet off the furniture, too.

If the family pet is your responsibility, be responsible.

Parents

If you are feeling the typical, "My mother (or father) is a pain, she just doesn't understand," reverse the role and YOU try to understand her (him).

Don't be ashamed of, or apologize for your way of life, your parents, your home, car, school, etc. Someone will always have more than you and someone will always have less.

If your parents do not dress the way some of your friends' parents do, it might be because they are putting you and your social needs FIRST. Be thankful, not shameful.

Remember special days such as your parents' anniversary, their birthdays, your younger sister's birthday. It's easy to remember Mother's Day and Father's Day.

For no reason at all, make someone else's day special.

Be loyal to your family. Be proud of your parents. If it weren't for them ...you know the rest.

General Rules for All Times, Wherever You May Be

Every time you step outside your house, you are making a public appearance. Sometimes you have a larger audience than other times.

- Walk with good posture. Speak in a low voice. There's no need to shout (includes cell phone), laugh loudly, sing, whistle or hum (unless of course you're one of the seven dwarfs).

- Don't make comments or talk to strangers.

- Don't lean against walls, put your feet on furniture or sit on the backs of anyone's couches or chairs.

- If you have trash, dispose of it properly.

- Keep your shoes on and avoid picking your nose, face or anything else.

- Remember that pretty girls and cows look alike when they chew gum...no gum chewing!

Babysitting

When you have committed to babysit for someone, you have accepted a responsible job. Imagine parents trusting you with their children. Be sure you want this responsibility before you accept.

Before the parents leave, all instructions should be perfectly clear to you, such as bedtime or if a child has to take medication. An emergency telephone number should be at hand. Also be aware of a number where the parents can be reached and where they are going.

Don't hit, yell or treat a child in a cruel way. This is NOT your responsibility. Never lock a child in a room.

Avoid off-color jokes, nasty language, threatening statements, spooky stories or anything that frightens a child.

If the parents offer you something to eat or drink, it's OK to help yourself. However, a mess is not left anywhere and you don't eat them out of house and home.

Don't clean house while you are babysitting. You are there to supervise the child.

If you have permission to use the telephone or watch television, do so *only* after the child is in bed. Don't give out the telephone number to your friends.

Read to a small child. Play with older children. Give them your "undivided" attention. After all, that's what you're being paid to do!

t School

Neatness and cleanliness count in school, too.

- Be cheerful and kind to everyone, even your classmates who may not be very nice to you, or who may be the class nerds.

- Your teachers are human. They enjoy a "good morning, good afternoon, have a nice evening" or just a smile.

- Open doors for others. Pick up something that someone drops.

- Avoid cliques, groups, or pairing off with "just one friend." all of the time. If you're not as popular as you would like to be, ask yourself why. Are you reaching out to be friends with others?

- Nice people have a built in loving kindness. They shun any opportunity to think, speak or act in a way that would damage another person's tastes, self-respect, pride, self-confidence and loyalties.

- You spend a lot of time at school. It's easier to abide by and obey the rules than rebel or try to make your own rules. The class clown ends up "not so funny" after a while.

- Be loyal to your school. Don't talk about your school policies or teachers in a negative way. Let your school be proud of you and the way you act in public.

Religious Services

Most religions have special occasion ceremonies that take place in a house of worship. When you're invited to attend a religious service other than that of your own faith, please abide by the following:

- Arrive on time.

- Be clean and neat. Wear your good clothes; no tennis shoes, jeans, or shorts.

- Stop talking before you enter and once you are inside avoid giggling, whispering, or telling jokes. This is not the time for gadgets, games, swinging your feet, or opening and closing your purse.

- Sit, stand, and participate in the service if you want to. However, skip rituals that may be foreign to you such as taking communion or immersing yourself in the baptismal font.

- If a collection basket or plate is passed around, it isn't for the taking. It's for members to contribute.

- Leave your beeper at home.

- If you have a gift for the honoree, send it to his home or give it to her at the party later. Don't bring it to the church or synagogue.

It is totally unthinkable to ever make fun of other people's religious beliefs. You must respect their beliefs and you can do this by paying attention. You might even learn something

Which are most important at a religious service?
❑ *silence*
❑ *respect*
❑ *attention*
❑ *promptness*
❑ *all of the above*

# 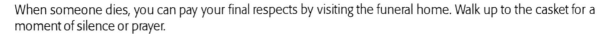akes and Funerals

When someone dies, you can pay your final respects by visiting the funeral home. Walk up to the casket for a moment of silence or prayer.

As you see members of the grieving family, express your sympathy by saying, "I am very sorry," or, "Please accept my sympathy." A hug or a handshake is an appropriate and comforting gesture.

This is a very difficult time and sometimes just being with a close friend and being willing to help in any way, means more than words.

A sympathy card with a nice note (hand)written (in ink) inside is always appropriate.

Your thoughtfulness during a time of sorrow is greatly appreciated and always remembered.

When someone loses a pet, it's also a nice gesture to call, make a visit or send a card to show your sympathy.

*Remember these
kind ways to express
your sympathy:*
- ❑ *offer of help*
- ❑ *a hug*
- ❑ *words of comfort*
- ❑ *personal note*
- ❑ *thoughtfulness*
- ❑ *call or visit*
- ❑ *silent prayer*

CHAPTER SIX

Put It In Writing

Thank You Notes

Even though you said "thank you," it's nice to put it in writing! A telephone call is not a substitute for a written note. A thank-you note is in order when someone gives you a gift, takes you somewhere, helps you with a project. In other words, whenever someone extends a courtesy or does something nice for you. Other times to write a thank-you note are when you've been a guest for a weekend or longer in someone's home; when you receive a gift for any occasion; if you've been sick and receive flowers or gifts. When in doubt whether to write a thank-you note, or not, *write it.* It's fine to err on the side of graciousness. A thank-you note should be written as soon as possible within 24 hours. When you write soon, your feelings will creep right into the note.

A thank-you note should be handwritten in ink. Colored ink is fine, but don't use a pencil. Forget the preprinted note. Say what you feel and let it come from your heart.

Dear...

What do you say in a thank-you note?

- Mention the gift or whatever it is you're thankful for.
- Proceed further and let the giver know what you plan to do with it or have done with it.
- Tell the person "how much" you like the gift or why you are so happy with it.
- Should you receive a gift you already have, let it remain your secret.
- If you're thanking someone for a gift you're not wild about, and can't find anything to say about it, thank the person for her *thoughtfulness.*

In a note to someone who has given you money, you don't have to mention the amount but do tell the person what you intend to spend it on.

Begin your note with "Dear." ☛ Dear Mary, Dear Mrs. Smith...

Keep nice margins and try to write as straight across the paper as you can so your note doesn't look babyish.

When you "close," which comes right after the body of your note or letter, sign "Love," and then your name under it.

Dear Aunt Helen

Thank you for the beautiful music box. It adds so much to my collection. I think of you in a special way every time I play it

Love, Jodi

Stationery

Informal ☛ An informal is a fold-over note card that may be used for thank-you notes. Your name or initials on the outside is nice! Open the informal and begin writing under the fold. If you have to continue, turn to the back of the informal.

Postcards ☛ Postcards are popular and may be personalized, decorative, colored or plain. They seem to speed things up a bit.

Correspondence Card ☛ A correspondence card is generally 4" x 6" in size and is also nice for writing thank-you notes, sending or replying to invitations. The correspondence card may have your name and address on it, but not too large or you won't have room for your note.

Notepaper ☛ Having notepaper with your name on it is nice. You need more room when writing a letter, so if you get to the bottom of the page, begin on page two. Do not turn your stationery over and write on the back.

Avoid scratching out, erasing or using a cover up solution. Write a practice note first and then copy it onto your paper after it is exactly the way you want it.

Letters

If you are writing a letter and have more than one page, the first page is on top, followed by the other pages.

☛ You may type or computer-print a letter but sign your name in ink.

☛ Sign your name so that it can be read.

Invitation

You may answer an invitation in writing. If you accept, repeat in your acceptance the time, date, and place. Add, too, that you are really looking forward to...

If you have to regret, you may simply state that you are unable to attend.

Envelopes

Your envelope may match your stationery, or it may be a coordinating color.

When you insert a letter in the envelope, fold the pages in half or thirds and place in your envelope folded side in first. An informal is placed in the envelope, folded side up.

A correspondence card is placed in the envelope, top in first.

When the correspondence comes out right side up, the reader doesn't have to turn it in every direction.

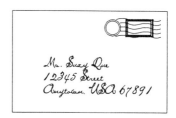

Address an envelope in three lines. Always use an honorific or a title.

Ms. Suzy Que
12345 Street
Anytown, USA 67891

Be sure your address is on the back of the envelope. The stamp goes in the upper right hand corner.

Correspondence

Greeting Cards

There are so many kinds of greeting cards. You don't really need an occasion to send a card! Everyone likes to be remembered with a card, especially on a birthday. Keep a list of your friends' birthdays.

☛ Remember your parents' wedding anniversary with a card. You might even want to make their card.

☛ If a friend's mother should be in the hospital, send her a card.

☛ If a friend's relative has died, send a sympathy card to the family.

☛ Your parents love to receive notes from you. Tuck one inside their suitcase when they go on a trip.

Be creative and design your cards on the computer, but always write a few lines on the inside of any card you send or enclose with a gift to give it a really personal touch.

E-Mail

In case you don't know what E-mail stands for, it is electronic mail. This means you may send letters, notes, messages by way of the Internet.

No two people have the same e-mail address. There's strict format (name@organization.domain) to e-mail addresses so use it.

E-mail is quick. You don't have to find a piece of paper, lick the envelope and look for a stamp. It makes it real easy to respond in a *not so nice way* to someone who has irritated you. Cool down before you electronically blurt out at someone.

If you ever wonder why you're not receiving notes, cards and letters from friends, it might be because you're not sending them. The same with e-mail...the more you send, the more you get.

Fax Machines

Another electronic device with the purpose of making our lives easier, *of course!*

When you fax someone, you are using their paper. Avoid sending a 25-page fax during the night, only to surprise the person the next morning with enough paper to wallpaper a room. Call the person first to make sure the machine is on or that it's even okay to send a fax.

Nothing is confidential with a fax, unless the person is standing over the machine waiting to grab it.

Do not fax thank-you notes, invitations, replies or letter of condolence. In other words, don't let the fax machine take the warmth, the human element, out of what you want to convey.

CHAPTER SEVEN

Beautiful You

$\mathcal{S}$kin Care

The best gift you can give yourself is a "clean" face! Your complexion will tell everyone "what" you eat and drink, "how much" exercise and sleep you get and even "how" you feel. In order to keep the smooth and delicate complexion you now have, basic skin care is essential. You will need the following:

- headband
- mild soap, or whatever your mother gives you
- washcloth
- towel
- mirror
- (of course) water

My skin is:
- ❏ *oily*
- ❏ *dry*
- ❏ *normal*

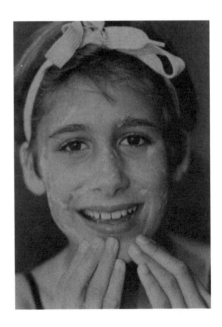

Put on your headband and pull all of your hair off your face. Bangs included. Now you're ready to cleanse. Here's what you do. Wet your hands, not a washcloth, with warm water and lather with mild soap. Here is the really important part. Use only your fingertips and make tiny circles going "up and out" all over your face. Watch in the mirror as you do this and go all the way out to your hairline.

Your skin LOVES water, therefore, give it a good splash with lukewarm to cool water. A washcloth may be used to rinse, if you do so in a gentle way. Be sure to remove every trace of soap. BLOT dry with a towel. Blot for beauty. Rubbing is O-U-T.

If you can cleanse in this manner twice a day - great! However, it is necessary that you cleanse properly before you go to bed at night. Keep pencils, hands, telephone receivers and anything else you can think of, off your face.

The Eyes Have It

If you have begun wearing a little eyeshadow or mascara, it has to come off before you go to bed at night. The five minutes extra sleep you get by not washing your face at night isn't worth the damage it will cause to your skin. Remove your eye makeup first because you don't want to smear it all over the rest of your face. Baby oil is a great substitute for eye makeup remover.

The most delicate area on your face is the area directly under your eyes. Don't pull or tug at it because once this part of your face is stretched out, it will never go back in place. Be as gentle with your under eye area as you would a pair of butterfly's wings. Guess why you should go "up and out" when washing your face? Because the older you get, gravity will begin forcing your skin to sag. There's no point in helping, so do just the opposite...always up and out.

As You Approach Puberty

As you get older, your hormones will begin to change and you may notice your face starting to break out. Don't be alarmed, it happens to everyone. There are three basic skin types. This is what to look for in determining your skin type.

- Oily   Looks shiny, feels moist
- Dry   Flaky, rough to touch
- Normal   Natural glow, feels smooth

Many pre-teens and teens have a combination skin type. The "T" zone, which is across your forehead and down the center of your face, is oily. The cheeks are dry.

Deep, Deep Cleansing

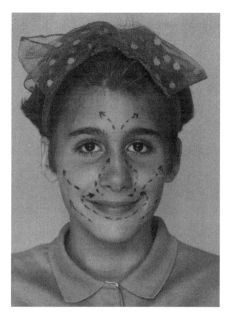

Surely, you've heard and seen someone use a "mud pack." This is simply a "deep cleanser." You can do the same thing with the following home remedy. Place a towel over your head, tent style, and bend over the bathroom sink while the hot water is running. You are now steaming your face, preparing it to be deep cleaned! In a small cup place some powdered milk, non-fat dry milk, and a little water until you create a paste consistency. Now spread this all over your face, again in an up and out motion except for the delicate area under your eyes. While this is hardening, relax. Place a couple of cucumber slices on your eyelids. Put your feet up. Read a book and don't be frightened when you look in the mirror.

After about 15 minutes it's time to remove the mask with cool water and a washcloth. *Remember: Up and Out.* Blot dry with a towel. Voila! Doesn't your skin feel new and totally refreshed. Your face may look like it's breaking out. This is normal because you are bringing all of the impurities to the surface. After a couple of times, your complexion will glow. It will look and feel great. Do this deep cleansing only once a week, no more.

What Do You Eat?

Unfortunately, more goes into having a lovely complexion than just keeping it clean. What you eat and drink is most important. The food pyramid should be your guide. Eating the right foods will give your body the fuel it needs while providing you with a beautiful complexion. Drink lots and lots of water. Real moisture comes from within your body.

A Sleeping Beauty

In addition to eating the proper foods and keeping your face clean, you should get at least 10-12 hours of sleep every night. This will avoid circles or bags under your young, pretty eyes. Your personality will be pleasant and happy because lack of sleep makes one grouchy and snappy. Hasn't your mother mentioned at some time that she has noticed this? And, hasn't it been after a pajama party or some unusual time when you were up most of the night?

Beauty Exercises Count

Everyone, even you, needs exercise every day. When your body is in tip-top condition, your skin is flawless, your hair gleams, fingernails are healthy, eyes sparkle and you will feel great. That's a promise! Walking is a super exercise. Develop good exercise habits now and they will stay with you forever. ▶

Have you ever noticed what a dog does when he gets up? He s-t-r-e-t-c-h-e-s and pulls every muscle in his body. Try this when you get up. Stretch every chance you get. You won't be sorry.

A Face Shape All Your Own

Before your can learn to highlight your good features and hide your not-so-good features through the use of makeup, hairstyling, colors, wardrobe and even accessories, you will have to know your face shape.

An "oval" is known as the perfect shaped face and the one you should strive for.

How do you find your particular face shape? Pull all of your hair off your face. Stand before a mirror and with a piece of soap in your hand, follow the outline of your face on the mirror. Now stand back. What shape or combination of shapes do you see?

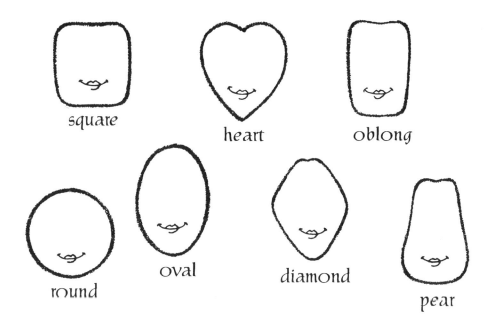

square

heart

oblong

round

oval

diamond

pear

My face shape is:
- ❏ *round*
- ❏ *oval*
- ❏ *square*
- ❏ *diamond*
- ❏ *heart*
- ❏ *oblong*
- ❏ *pear*

Eating Nutritiously

It seems that overnight your body has changed. You look in the mirror and you DO see someone different... and you feel different too!

For many of you weight control will become a life long worry and concern, if you let it. It is important to remember that starving yourself is not the way to get your weight in control.

Eating sensibly and exercising daily controls weight.

BEWARE: There are no magical tricks to eating. Dieting is a dangerous adventure. You may do harm to your body such as stopping growth, weakening your muscles and much more. You want to eat for health. What is healthy?

It's so simple. You need to eat foods that are loaded with NUTRIENTS not calories. If you eat foods from the food pyramid you will be eating a balanced diet. If you eat less or cut back, you end up the loser in health not in weight control. Here's what the food pyramid can do for you.

Recommended Daily Servings
USDA Food Pyramid

- Meat, Fish and Legumes

    This group provides protein and fat. Without protein and fat you stop growing. You develop colds easily. Your muscles weaken. Your fingernails begin to break. Your hair becomes dull, listless and even falls out.

- Fruits and Vegetables

    This group provides vitamins and minerals that NO "vitamin pill" can begin to provide. Without vitamins like A and C your skin becomes dry and scaly. Your vision is not as sharp at night. Your gums become sore and bleed.

- Milk and Cheese

    Calcium is the mineral that is found in this group. Calcium is so important for your bones now and as you become an adult. Without enough calcium your teeth loosen and decay easily. The bones along your spine weaken and you develop a curved back. Good posture exercises won't straighten a back that is deficient in calcium.

- Bread, Grains and Cereals

> This group provides energy for your mind and body. Without carbohydrates in your diet you become tired, weak, moody. Your concentration span is shortened.

Listen to your body. It will give you signals. Be alert to what is best for *your* body...not your friend's. With proper nutrition and diet you win at the game of losing! Keep your portions small. DO NOT deprive yourself of "junk" foods; anything in moderation is fine.

Exercise daily. You will be able to hold your weight steady until you have grown up. Not only will you be in control of your eating as a teenager but also as an adult. All the false promises in the world can't replace sensible eating.

Nature's most basic and best beauty secret is eating well. Try it, you'll like it!

 Pretty Smile

A lovely complexion goes hand in hand with a pretty smile. You need shining teeth for a beautiful smile. These are the years you will have the most cavities; so brush, brush, brush correctly and often. Flossing also helps remove soft particles of food that brushing can't reach. Your dentist will show you the correct ways to brush and floss.

If you can't brush between meals, an apple is a great tooth cleaner. One student thought this meant she didn't have to brush anymore, but eat apples instead! Wrong.

Of course your teeth are for chewing, but *only* food. This means such things as fingernails, erasers, pencils, clips and GUM stay out of your mouth. There is nothing pretty about watching or listening to someone chew gum.

Gum chewing is for cows (even the sugarless) and not pretty ladies. Have you ever seen a pretty cow?

Braces are temporary and with great rewards.

Breathtaking

Sweet smelling breath is a beauty necessity. Keep your mouth immaculately clean by proper brushing and flossing. Brush your tongue, too. Use a mouthwash, if need be and keep mints handy if you have a sinus problem, cold, allergy or might have eaten something spicy.

 A Crown on Your Head

Your hair will shine like a "crown on your head," if it is clean, healthy and well cared for. This is the only way it will collect compliments for you.

Shampoo Often

It's OK to shampoo as often as you like, but a *must* is once a week. Follow the steps below for shampooing properly:

- Brush your hair thoroughly. Remove all tangles.

- Soak your combs and brushes in warm water and shampoo.

- Wet your hair with warm water.

- Lather your entire scalp with your favorite shampoo.

- Make a fist with each hand and use *only your knuckles,* ▶ not your fingernails, to massage your scalp.

- Rinse thoroughly.

- Lather again and this time clean your hair instead of your scalp.

- Rinse again.

- Now the squeak test. Take a small amount of your hair and pull it through your fingers. Listen for a squeak because this is your signal that your hair is clean and all the soap is gone.

- Apply a conditioner or cream rinse, if you use one. Then rinse for the final time.

- Wrap your hair in a towel, turban style.

- Rinse your combs and brushes and let them dry, bristles down.

- BLOT your hair dry. Don't rub because this may cause split ends. (See photo, opposite.)

- Use a "wide tooth" comb and begin combing from the bottom and go toward your scalp. Combing from the top down, which is what you probably have been doing, will eventually ruin your hair. Never pull a tangle from the top of your scalp to the bottom. (More than the tangle will come out.)

Wet Head

If possible, let your hair dry naturally, even if only for a few minutes. Don't blow dry soaking wet hair. Weather permitting, go outside and let your hair dry naturally. Towel dry your hair before you apply a gel or mousse.

Blow Drying

When blow drying your hair, avoid "baking" any one particular area or section. Instead, keep your dryer moving. Hold your dryer at least 6" away from your hair.

Hold your hair straight out with your styling brush and gently move the dryer back and forth. For a fuller look, blow dry your hair in the "opposite" direction and then brush it into the style you want.

Brushing

There are all sorts of brushes on the market and you probably have your fair share of them. There are natural bristle brushes, rubber tipped brushes, nylon bristle brushes and combinations thereof. It makes no difference which one you choose. Just be certain the bristles are rounded and not sharp.

Keep all of your brushes in a drawer when not in use since they tend to collect dirt and dust.

To Curl or Not

If you curl your own hair, be careful not to burn yourself with a curling iron (or heat rollers). Hold a small portion of your hair out to the side. Place the clamp of the curling iron on the very ends of your hair now roll it under, clamp is on top, and hold for a few seconds. Open the clamp and remove the iron. If you do not get the very ends of your hair, you will create a bend which is called a fish hook. The only way to get rid of a fish hook is to wet your hair. Roll your hair in the direction you want the curl.

To Each His Own

You NEVER EVER borrow or lend a comb or brush to anyone. This just invites trouble in the form of dandruff and whatnot. Dandruff is bad enough, but the "whatnot" is worse.

Your Kind of Hair

Some types of hair will perform much better than others. Some will need more time on your part. Which of the following applies to you?

- **Fine**   shiny, silky, flyaway, won't hold curl
- **Coarse**   thick, feels heavy, holds curl well
- **Medium**   sometimes responds like fine; other times like coarse hair

Is your hair curly, wavy or straight? Here's a test to tell you. Shampoo your hair, comb it out and let it dry naturally (no blow drying, combing or brushing). You will see:

- **Straight**   no curl, but may turn up or under at ends
- **Wavy**   shows S-curves in some places or all over
- **Curly**   may be ringlets or frizz, hard to comb

Now decide one of the following:

- **Oily**   looks limp and dirty
- **Dry**   looks dull, no bounce, flaky
- **Normal**   great balance

Understand your hair's natural characteristics and you will have more fun working with it. But what about changing hairstyles?

Which Style For You

Certain features you have to live with such as your ears, nose, mouth, eyes, but *not* your hair. Only you can control how it looks and a hairstyle does not have to be complicated to be pretty.

Try various looks. Braids, asymmetrical, pony tail, ribbons, cellophane, yarn, headband, can all be exciting.

Look through magazines and find a hairstyle you like. Whenever you see someone with a hairstyle your like, ask her where she gets it cut. Maybe your mother has a hairstylist she likes and you will, too. So, find a hairstylist who will listen to you, look at your picture and work with you. They are few and far between but well worth the hunt.

The key is to have your hairstylist cut your hair and show you how to take care of it in between visits.

Ladyfingers

There is nothing you can do about the size of your hands or shape of your fingers but you can keep them groomed and use them as gracefully as possible.

Treat your fingernails like precious jewels. Protect them with rubber gloves when you are doing certain chores. Avoid using your fingernails to pry things open or for a tool to dig into something. Use your fingertip not your fingernail to dial a telephone. Use knuckles for scrubbing your scalp not fingernails.

If you choose to wear fingernail polish, it must be ALL on or ALL off. In other words, chipped nail polish is not permitted under any circumstance. Your nails are better bare than polish that's barely there!

Wear gloves in the winter to protect your hands from the cold. If your hands should become chapped or rough, apply hand cream and sleep in white cotton gloves.

I have only three words for girls who bite their fingernails - STOP, STOP, STOP.

Biting your fingernails will cause them to be jagged and ugly. Only you can control this habit. It is neither pretty nor polite to bite your fingernails. Instead, eat an apple, work on a craft, read a book. Not interested in doing any of these things then SIT on your hands.

- For graceful hands, lead with your wrist whenever you reach for anything.

- Wriggle and shake your fingers to loosen them.

- Another exercise for prettier hands is to *fist and stretch*.
  Make a fist, fingers tucked in, open your hands and s-t-r-e-t-c-h.

Fingertips

Your fingernails will snitch on you! No matter how good the rest of you looks, you cannot get away with chewed up, messy, dirty fingernails. Every morning check to see that your nails are sparkling clean. Once a week give yourself a manicure. Allow plenty of time. Enjoy!

Gather the following:

- a bowl of warm water mixed with a little shampoo
- manicure mat (towel, Kleenex, napkin)
- cotton balls
- emery board
- nail polish remover

- cuticle remover
- orangewood stick
- tooth pick
- buffer or nail polish
- lots of time

Which is not used in a manicure?
- ❏ *emery board*
- ❏ *orange stick*
- ❏ *tooth pick*
- ❏ *bread stick*
- ❏ *buffer*
- ❏ *warm water*

Unfold your Kleenex or napkin and use it as a manicure mat. Saturate a cotton ball with remover and press it on your nail rather than rubbing it. If you have polish in the cuticle use a cotton swab or toothpick to remove it.

File your fingernails with an emery board. A metal file may cause your nails to split. Hold your hand toward you while you file and you may file in both directions. Be careful not to file too closely to the sides of your nails or you will cause hangnails and they hurt!

Your fingernails should all be about the same length. Save the claws for ferocious animals, not pretty ladies.

Your cuticle is the little ridge of thick skin at the base of each nail. Apply cuticle remover if you have it, to your cuticles. Now push them back with the orange stick. Never cut your cuticles, as they will become sore.

Soak your fingers in your bowl of sudsy water. By the way, hair shampoo is used because your fingernails and hair are made of the same protein called keratin.

Scrub with your fingernail brush to remove any grim or loose cuticle.

Dry your nails and cuticles with the towel. Whenever you dry your hands, push your cuticles back with the towel. It only takes a second.

A smidge of baby oil or Vaseline on your cuticles every night before going to bed will keep them soft.

Nail polish protects your nails.

- ☛ Shake your bottle of nail polish or roll it between your fingers to distribute the polish before opening it.
- ☛ Apply it starting at the base going all the way to the tip of your nail.
- ☛ Three long strokes will give you an even finish.
- ☛ If you should get nail polish in your cuticle, use a toothpick to remove it.

Nail polish remover will NOT thin your polish. Instead keep your nail polish in the refrigerator so you can use it to the last drop.

Let your nails dry thoroughly. Even if you use a spray or quick dry, allow yourself enough time because your polish will nick unless it's totally dry.

If you prefer buffing for a pretty shine instead of polish that's OK, too. A shine is always appropriate. Smooth hand cream going toward your wrists.

Beautiful nails require which of the following:
- ❑ *non-chipped polish*
- ❑ *gloves in winter*
- ❑ *nail biting*
- ❑ *hand exercises*
- ❑ *delicate treatment*

Footworks

Your feet. They support your body and carry you around all day everyday, therefore, they too need special care. Most young ladies forget their feet. They squash them into shoes that don't fit. Feet are stepped on, underprotected and overworked.

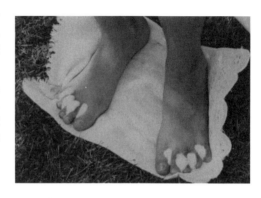

If your shoes fit properly, you will avoid calluses, corns, blisters and other foot problems. Buy your shoes at the end of the day, after school, when your feet are most swollen. Avoid shoes that have to be "broken in" before they are comfortable If your shoes are too tight and your feet hurt, it will show up in your eyes.

Feet First

Follow the manicure steps to give yourself a "pedicure." In warm weather your feet are more visible so treat yourself to a pedicure once every two weeks. In the winter, once a month is fine.

Use a nail clipper to clip your nails straight across. Do not dig into the sides. An emery board will smooth your nails.

Apply a "light" polish to your toenails. Dark or bright polish will draw attention to your feet. Most of the time a clear or neutral polish looks best on your toenails.

Put cotton between your toes to keep your toenails separated while they are drying.

Treat for Your Feet

Walking barefoot on sand is great as the sand works as a pumice to soften feet. Walking barefoot on a hard surface hardens skin and promotes calluses.

Use plenty of body lotion on your feet. Bath powder rubbed between your toes for a quick picker upper. Be kind to your feet; they take you wherever you want to go.

Your Beauty Bath

RELAX! Set aside enough time for one of the most heavenly pleasures on earth - a long, luxurious, relaxing bath.

A shower definitely gives you a zippy pickup but a "beauty bath" does so much more! Go ahead and treat yourself.

Gather your supplies before stepping in the tub. You will need soap, a washcloth, backbrush, fingernail brush, loofa sponge, mirror, large fluffy towel. Oh, yes and a book if you enjoy reading. You will NOT need your cell phone, beeper, hairdryer or anything electrical.

Begin running your bath water and I can assure you that any temperature your toe can stand, your bottom can stand! Go for the warm.

How about a "milk bath." I once thought that meant pouring milk in the water. It doesn't!

Here is a recipe:

- ☛ Take an old, clean stocking and fill the toe with uncooked, dry, oatmeal. Tie a knot to hold the oatmeal.

- ☛ Now swish this stocking back and forth in the water. It will turn a milky color. This is a wonderful way to soften your skin. You may use it over and over again.

- ☛ Just squeeze the stocking when you're finished and place it in a little dish until next time. A couple drops of baby oil will also keep your skin soft.

Step in, lie back and think marvelous thoughts. You did remember to pull your hair up and off your face? If bathtub singing is your idea of fun, chirp away. Reading to catch up on? Now is the time.

Enough Relaxation!

Now it's time to get down to some serious business. First, your face. Cleanse in the manner we previously discussed.

- ☛ Then there are your ears (inside and out), neck, elbows and feet. It's easy to forget those places. Use your loofa sponge on your elbows and feet. Your manicure brush will come in handy for your fingernails and toenails.

- ☛ Rinse well, with clean water. Reach for your fluffy towel and pat dry.

- ☛ Dip into a box of dusting powder. Dust from limb to limb and don't forget "between your toes."

- ☛ Apply a body lotion all over your body making sure a generous portion is placed on your elbows, knees and heels. Splash on your favorite fragrance. Spray it in an "up and down" pattern and then step through it.

Please clean up the bathroom. Make sure there is no "ring around the bathtub." Take your dirty clothes and wet towel and put them where they belong.

Plan a beauty bath about once a week. Be sure the bathroom is all yours because you don't want to "rush." A bath or shower is a daily must.

Defuzzing

When the hair on your legs and underarms is visible, it's time to begin shaving. However, once you start you must be stubble-free forever. For some of you, this means shaving daily; for others, it might be every other day.

An electric or battery operated razor is all you'll need in the beginning. If a safety razor is your choice, lather the area to be shaved with shaving cream, which is not as drying as soap. Gently glide the razor, either kind, opposite your hair growth. The best time to shave with an electric razor is right before your bath or shower.

A safety razor may be used in the shower or bathtub. Never shave your arms or any hair on your face. There are specific hair lighteners for these areas.

Powder under your arms after shaving. Your skin is especially sensitive after shaving. Deodorant might burn.

Deodorant

Daily use of a deodorant is a must. Apply in a circle, covering your entire under arm area. Apply deodorant after your daily shower or bath.

Making Sense of Scents

The finishing touch in beauty is fragrance. Experiment with different perfume scents. Pretty soon you'll find one you really like. When you do, get the bath powder and body lotion in the same scent.

There are florals, spices, orientals, fruits and many other blends. Don't let your nose be the judge when you smell a perfume on someone else because every fragrance will be different on every single person.

- To test a fragrance, apply a few drops to your inner wrist. Allow them to dry, then sniff. This first impression is the "top note." Wait about 10 minutes and sniff your wrist again.

- There will be a difference because the fragrance is beginning to blend with your body chemistry. This is the "middle note."

- In about two or three hours you will notice a lingering aroma. This is the "bottom note" and what will be obvious to others.

Rank the following in order of fragrance strength:
__ cologne
__ eau de toilette
__ perfume

Perfume has the most fragrance oil, therefore, more concentrated and stronger than other forms of fragrance. It is also the most expensive.

Eau de toilette is second in strength because it has more alcohol and water than fragrance oil.

Cologne has the least amount of fragrance oil. Your fragrance should not be overpowering.

Apply your fragrance to your pulse points after your shower or bath because your body is still warm and all fragrances cling better to a warm body. Your pulse points are your temples, wrists, base of your throat, inner arms at your elbow, back of knees.

In the warm weather keep your cologne in the refrigerator for an extra refreshing splash.

Avoid applying any fragrance to your clothing or furs, should you be so lucky!

When you are finished with a bottle of your favorite fragrance, take the lid off and store it in your lingerie drawer. Looking for a great pick me upper, spray or splash on your favorite scent anytime of the day.

CHAPTER EIGHT

Looking Good

Fashion Sense

Rich or poor, fat or skinny, tall or short, all are faced with the same problem. How to choose the clothes that will make you look your prettiest. Some girls can wear ruffles and frills while others look better in more tailored clothing; still others may be adventurous in their choices.

Keep pace with fashion, but let your own personality and physical characteristics be your first consideration. What looks good on one of your friends may not look good on you. Be honest with yourself.

The most important rule in dressing smartly is simplicity. Haven't you ever noticed someone who has "too much" of everything on? You will develop your own style, what you like and what looks best on you, as you become more and more interested in clothes.

As important as clothing is, YOU want to be remembered for you and not what you wore. For instance, a nice compliment would be, "You look great in that color" rather than, "What a great looking color."

About Color

Everyone has a favorite color or colors. Your eyes, hair and skin tone play an important role in choosing the "right" colors for you. Again, you will learn this in time.

Some colors will make you look glamorous. Other colors will change your facial coloring or hair; some make you look older. Dark colors make you look smaller in size while light or bright colors will enlarge. And, certain colors go better together than others.

Colors have personalities just like you do. For instance, orange is very exciting; yellow is sunny and gay; blue is very cool; green is restful and quiet; red is warm and friendly, while purple is quite royal. If you wear red or bright yellow on a real hot day, you look and, no doubt, feel warm. How do some other colors make you feel? Try a bright, sunny color on a rainy, dreary day to change your mood.

What to Wear

Dress appropriately. Do not overdress. If you're going to a picnic or barbecue, wear a sporty outfit such as shorts, knickers, slacks or a sundress. A rhinestone-studded, denim jacket and cutoff jeans, probably won't impress your grandmother at a family reunion.

If you are going to a birthday party, wear a dressier dress. Party dresses are for special occasions and celebrations. When you're unsure of the dress code and unable to find out, wear a simple "go everywhere dress."

School clothes are for school, NOT for play or dress. Play clothes are rough and tough and are for play only. Jeans should not be worn to a house of worship. Neither are your favorite, oversized t-shirts, which make a statement across the front. However, these are great nightshirts!

Any garment rumpled or wrinkled, even though it may be a hot fashion item, gives the impression you spent the last twenty minutes in the dryer being tumbled dry. There are times and places for looks like these one of which is not parents' night at your school.

If in doubt, your mother will help you decide what is appropriate. She will be honest with you, too.

Dress, coat, hat, jewelry, handbag and shoes worn at the same time should all be in the same category: casual, dressy, school, play. For instance, you do not wear good patent shoes with a pair of jeans. Or plastic jewelry and play shoes with a fancy party dress.

Lines and Designs

The fabric, or what the garment is made of, generally determines how dressy or casual it is rather than the style, which means how it's made. Keep your size in mind when choosing patterns or prints in a fabric. If you're a large girl you can lean toward the larger prints. A small or petite girl should stay with smaller patterns.

No one should wear HUGE polka dots, plaids or stripes. (Put these on your walls.) Since you're still growing don't worry too much about this now.

- ☛ Vertical lines || up and down   make you look taller
- ☛ Horizontal lines   =   around   make you look shorter
- ☛ Asymmetrical   //   diagonal   make you look thinner

Perfect Fit

Your clothing should fit properly. Nothing is more uncomfortable or looks worse than a dress or pair of slacks that are either too small or too large. So when mother tells you something no longer fits, and it may be your favorite, listen to her and put it to rest.

Underneath It All

You must change your undies every single day. One time, many years ago, I was speaking to a group of ten-year-old young ladies and when I mentioned they must change their underwear every single day, one little darling replied, "Why? No one sees it."

Undershirt, slip or bra straps should be on your shoulders, not slipping off. Tugging at underpanties is a "no no" so make sure they fit or they will be uncomfortable. Avoid rolling a half slip up at the waist. It's better to purchase a smaller size. Have you ever noticed someone pulling her slip up at the waist, right there in front of everyone?

Under a see through blouse or sweater, you wear a slip, camisole, teddy or undershirt. Get in the habit of wearing flesh colored underwear. Flowers and stripes are cute on toddlers, but a flesh tone goes better under everything, especially white.

When it's time to wear a bra, don't be embarrassed. Instead, go to the lingerie department of a reputable department store and let the experienced salesperson help you. If your bra is incorrectly fitted your bust will not look natural.

Your Figure

It can be difficult to "figure" out exactly what shape your figure is in. There are two ways of checking. The first one is to put on your swimsuit and a bag over your head (cut out two holes for your eyes). Now stand before a full-length mirror. What do you see? Be honest.

Do you see a skinny, straight up and down, stringbean figure? Or maybe one that is a little too round all over, like an orange. Possibly your tummy or hips stick out a little too much and remind you of a pear. Are you tiny and petite? Could be you're "just right."

Another way to analyze your figure is to hang a huge piece of paper, or an old sheet, on the wall. Now ask your mother or best friend to outline your "ins and outs" with a thick marker. Stand back and take a look. Do you like what you see? Is the result lovely or do you have work to do?

Accessories

Less is Best! Accessories are the little extras that "make" your outfit. They can make it pretty, ugly, simple, gaudy or just right. Accessories, all of them, must be kept in proportion to your size. The occasion plays a part in accessorizing an outfit. Accessories include, but are not limited to, the following items:

Belts: Anytime self belt loops appear on a skirt, dress, slacks or shorts, a belt is needed and must be worn. The little crochet belt loops that are sewn on your dress should be carefully removed. It's not necessary to always wear the belt that comes with an outfit. Your whole look will change with a different belt. This is fun to do, too. A belt should be worn loose enough so that you can comfortably put your hand between the belt and your waistline. A too tight belt is unattractive and uncomfortable.

Jewelry: Your jewelry, like your clothing, should be chosen with care. Enameled, fun or "fake" jewelry is everyday or casual. Save your "good" jewelry, the "real" thing, for dressier times. Be very careful when wearing your (or your mother's) good jewelry so that you don't lose it.

If you put on pierced earrings while looking in a mirror over the bathroom sink, CLOSE the drain first. Should you lose a pierced earring save the other one and use it as a pin on a dress or collar. As soon as you take off your earrings, put the backings on them.

Unless you know how to mix metals so they don't look gaudy, wear all the same kind rather than mixing metals. This means gold with gold, silver with silver not silver with brass and so on. Pearls may be worn with any metal and should be worn for dressy times.

One ring on each hand is fine. When you put a ring on every finger, it's a bit much and none of your rings are noticed. There's no need to wear your whole jewelry box at one time.

Hats: Hats can change the look of an entire outfit, especially pretty straw hats in the spring. In the cold you can wear hats to keep warm as well as being fashionable.

Gloves: Gloves dress up an outfit from leather to lace. Light or white gloves must be clean; there are no exceptions. Put your gloves in your coat pocket or purse when you're out so you don't lose them. One glove really isn't worth much!

Which are accessory mistakes?
- ❏ *tight belt*
- ❏ *lots of rings*
- ❏ *mixing jewelry metals*
- ❏ *stuffed handbags*
- ❏ *worn shoes*
- ❏ *baggy socks*
- ❏ *hose with runners*
- ❏ *all above*

Handbags: Your handbag doesn't have to "match" your shoes, but it certainly should coordinate and blend with your outfit. Avoid "stuffing" your handbag. Bulges are not pretty anywhere. A shoulder bag will end at your hips, drawing attention to them. If your strap is too long, knot it before putting it over your shoulder. A clutch bag is carried in your hand, not under your arm. A book bag or backpack is carried the best way you can. All bags should be held in place, not swinging from side to side.

Avoid putting your purse on the table. It belongs on the chair with you, or on the floor next to you, but not on the table in a restaurant. If you're in the habit of forgetting your bag somewhere or asking your mother to hold it for you, then you need not carry one.

Shoes: When you're all dressed up wear your leather or patent leather pumps. White shoes are for summer as are most sandals. Tennis shoes are mostly for gym and play. Loafers, oxfords, brogues, topsiders and shoes along these lines are casual or school shoes. The heels and soles of your shoes should not look worn. White shoes must be white. Learn to polish your own shoes. Vaseline is great for putting a shine on patent leathers. After wearing a pair of shoes, dab the insides with alcohol and cotton to freshen them up a bit before putting them away. Sprinkle some talcum powder inside your tennis shoes. Oh, and a shoehorn will eliminate bending the heel of your shoes.

Please, please make sure your shoes fit and feel comfortable when your mother purchases them. Don't wait until you have to wear them to school or a special event and then happen to mention they don't fit!!! Besides, when your feet hurt, it shows up in your eyes.

Socks: Knee socks are worn at the knee, not falling to your ankles. Any sock edged with lace are for dress as are lacy and patterned pantyhose. Cables, knits, argyles and multi-color socks or tights are for casual or school. Tights, pantyhose, and stockings must not have runners, snags or be dirty.

Put It All Together

A final check before a full length mirror. Slip showing? Hem hanging properly? Too much jewelry? Collar clean? Just like manners, your clothes are one of the ways people will judge you.

DETAILS COUNT!

Wardrobe Inventory

Your room represents YOU. Therefore, it should be kept clean and tidy at all times. It's your responsibility to make your bed in the morning and to make sure all of your dirty clothes are where they belong. Take your clothes out and plan what you are going to wear the night before. Your morning will go much smoother. An organized room projects an organized young lady. Enough room preaching, let's get on with your closet and drawers.

Closet Makeover

A great idea twice a year is to take a wardrobe inventory, or a count of your clothing. This means to clean out your closet and drawers and make note of what you have, which will tell you what you need for an upcoming season. Take an inventory in the fall and spring of each year.

What you really need depends on your lifestyle. If you go to a lot of parties, you will need several party dresses. If you go to a parochial school, you probably wear uniforms and not need a variety of school clothes. On the other hand, if you attend a public school, you will need a lot of school clothes. Away we go!

Take everything out of your closet. Pick up each item and look at it. Ask yourself these questions:

Does it fit? Do I like it? Did I wear it last year?

- ☛ If you "YES" to all three of these questions, then put the garment in pile ONE.
- ☛ If you answer "no" then you have two choices. The first is to get rid of it. These garments go in pile TWO.
- ☛ The second choice is to save it, for whatever reason. This is pile THREE.

After everything is sorted, here's what you do.

- ☛ Everything in pile ONE goes back in your closet.
- ☛ Everything in pile TWO is put in a trash bag and given away Give it to a neighbor, charitable organization or throw it away. It makes no difference how you get rid of it, just do so.
- ☛ Everything in pile THREE is placed in a storage box and stored somewhere OTHER than your closet. Use the basement, attic or a storage closet.

So far so good! The only clothing you're concerned with now is what went back in your closet. Count the garments and use the inventory sheet in this book as you put them away.

As you put everything back, do it in an organized fashion. Hang your skirts together, dresses together, blouses together, slacks together. Leave a small space between each garment so nothing gets crushed.

Remember, anything you didn't wear one year, you won't wear the next so out it goes.

The Mix Up

Try mixing and matching your clothes. Take a blouse and see how many skirts, jumpers or slacks you can wear with it. Then the next time you feel you don't have anything wear, stand back and take a good look.

Getting Organized

Keep all of your shoes together either on a shoe rack or in their original shoe boxes with labels. This way they can be stacked on top of each other and still be easy to find. Surely you're not guilty of flinging your shoes off your feet into the closet and wherever they land is its final destination...a good way to scratch your shoes.

All of your belts should be in one place, too. Use a belt hanger or little hooks in your closet. Slip "matching" belts over the hanger of the specific garment.

List Below Your Clothing	School		Dress		Casual	
	Have	Need	Have	Need	Have	Need
Coats						
Jackets						
Blazers						
Blouses						
Sweaters						
Sweatshirts						
Skirts						
Slacks						
Jeans						
Shorts						
Warm-ups						
Jumpers						
Dresses						
Shoes						
Handbags						
Belts						
Earrings						
Bracelets						
Necklaces						
Scarves						
Hats						
Gloves						
Stockings						
Socks						
Slips						
Other						

All of your handbags should be together. One suggestion is to put them in a large plastic box on your shelf. This way you can see what's in the box. Another suggestion is a nine compartment cardboard shoe box that you can find in any department or discount store. Again, your handbags are visible. Shoulder bags can also hang on little hooks.

Place coats, jackets and dresses on sturdy hangers. Dresses should go on padded hangers. Pants and skirts should be placed on their appropriate hangers in order to keep them hanging wrinkle free.

Button all buttons, zip all zippers and empty all pockets before hanging any garment.

Do not hang knits or sweaters. They should be folded and stored on a shelf or in a drawer. If you hang a sweater, it will "grow" (stretch out of shape).

Stitch In Time

If a seam has ripped, hem come out or a button popped off, be sure to inform your mother so she can mend it before you need it again.

If what you just wore has to be dry-cleaned, put it where your mother has dry-cleaning. If it has to be laundered, then place it in the laundry basket.

If a garment doesn't need immediate attention after wearing it, let it air out before putting it in your closet.

*A winning
wardrobe is:*
❑ *coordinated*
❑ *organized*
❑ *laundered*
❑ *tidy*
❑ *current*
❑ *all of above*

Drawers, Too

As for your drawers, whether lingerie, dresser, chest or vanity, they should be neat and organized also.

If you do not have drawer dividers, they are fun to make by covering old shoeboxes with wrapping paper or matching wallpaper.

Now you may store your undershirts, slips, bras, underpants in separate compartments. Your socks may be separated by school, dress, play or even by color!

Your ribbons, barrettes and hair articles should be kept together in a special place in a drawer. Use little earring or gift boxes to make compartments. Again, be creative and cover them. Or how about an ice cube tray? It makes a wonderful organizer for your pierced earrings, chains, pins and smaller items. How terrible when you are in a hurry and a chain is tangled with another necklace or bracelet or you cannot find the back to an earring. Haste makes waste!

Put your hair dryer, curling iron, hairspray, gels IN something out of sight.

Everyone needs at least one junk drawer, shelf or box just for those items without a home. Every now and them clean it out and find a specific place for everything or discard what you don't want. In the meantime, it helps to keep clutter "out of the way."

Borrowing

Borrowing something, anything, is not a good habit to get into. However, if you must, then return whatever it was you borrowed in the exact condition in which it was lent to you.

Clothing must be laundered or dry-cleaned before you return it. If it tears, breaks or gets lost, it's your responsibility to replace it.

And, you only wear or use it for the purpose intended. Avoid hanging it in your closet for six months. Return the item as soon as possible.

A "thank-you" note accompanies the returned item.

If you want to discourage your friends from borrowing tell them your mother doesn't approve.

Neatness Counts

You will stand out and always look right when you're neat about yourself and organized within. Sloppiness also stands out in a crowd...but who wants to be remembered that way?

CHAPTER NINE

Pretty And Poised

Visual Poise

What does "visual poise" mean to you...?

Give up? The word *visual* refers to things that can be seen, and *poise* allows any situation to be handled with confidence. Therefore "visual poise" means doing smoothly and assuredly everything that anyone sees you do, such as the way you stand, sit, walk, or even pick up a book you've dropped.

Someone with poise is always calm. It hurts when you don't receive an invitation to a birthday party, or don't get the part you'd been practicing for in the school play (and your best friend gets it instead...). It's disappointing, but life goes on. You have to show you're happy for others and be gracious in your behavior toward everyone. If you feel like discussing your hurt feelings, have a heart-to-heart talk with your mother or father. You'll be surprised at how many similar experiences they went through—and lived to tell. (They really *were* your age once.) Anyway, no one will even remember (or care to) in 10 years; what seems like such a big deal now quickly fades from memory.

With poise on your side, you can handle any situation with ease. Poise seems stiff, but it's really exactly the opposite because it allows you to be flexible. If skyscrapers and church steeples weren't constructed to withstand winds and storms, they would collapse. A poised person is able to bend, make adjustments, and accept the unexpected without collapsing. When life serves you lemons, make lemonade. Remember Cinderella? She handled her situation with poise and look how it turned out...

Visual Poise in Daily Life

Visual Poise is related to so many parts of your physical being. For instance, your posture and figure are essential components of a graceful walk. The most carefully chosen wardrobe won't look good unless it's worn with grace of body. Self-confidence is evident in your personality, which has much to do with your personal appearance. A lovely face and a great hairstyle are only properly appreciated if above a perfectly erect body.

All facets of poise are interdependent...the more poised you are, the more poised you become. "Poise and Grace" are twins! When a lady is poised, she is confident. When she is graceful, her movements tell the whole world she is confident.

So What Is Confidence?

Confidence is a feeling, like happiness, love, joy. Confidence is the way you feel when you get an "A" on a test. Or the feeling you had when you were elected to the student council. Maybe you scored higher than anyone in your gymnastics class. This is the same feeling you have when you're confident about all situations. Imagine this. You must give a speech, before your whole school. You're dressed properly. Your nails are manicured and look pretty. Your hair is just the way you like it. Of course you know your material, so you are ready for everyone to see. You feel good about yourself. In fact you feel as though you could even conquer the world. This IS Confidence. You have a glow about you that everyone can see, when you are confident. However, no one is born confident. You must build your own from within.

Confidence, along with poise, belongs to every age. They can be learned at any time, but the sooner you begin to develop poise and confidence, the sooner you will discover their rewards. Nothing can stop you from gaining confidence. Once you achieve that faith in yourself, it will continue to grow as you grow. The one confidence you have the more you want.

Confidence Versus Conceit

"She is really conceited." "That girl has confidence." Have your heard these phrases before? Everyone has, but most of my students don't know the difference. Do you? Conceit is very different from confidence. The person who has to have everything her way, who is at a loss without constant praise and shattered by the least setback is not confident, merely conceited...bet you can think of someone who fills those shoes.

Confidence is genuine, the real thing. You are happy and comfortable with yourself and others are comfortable with you.

Conceit is artificial, not real. The conceited person is unsure of herself. She lacks self esteem, which means she does not like the kind of person she is. The girl who is nearly in tears because no one compliments her on her new fingernail polish, is conceited. The conceited person has to be complimented and pampered continuously. Of course, she never pays you a compliment because she is too busy thinking about herself to seek out the good in others. Besides, "no compliment" IS a compliment from some people! Friends do not come easy to the conceited person.

The confident person's strength comes from within. She believes in herself. She will always attract friends. After all, you must like yourself before you can expect anyone else to like you.

A positive attitude is one that says constantly, "I am, I can, I will." Remember the little engine that could?

Which are traits of confidence, not conceit?
- ❑ *poise*
- ❑ *feeling good*
- ❑ *low self-esteem*
- ❑ *selfishness*
- ❑ *needing praise*

The difference between a "SOMETHING" and a nothing is: C•O•N•F•I•D•E•N•C•E

You are unique, a very special person. There is NO ONE exactly like you (even though your grandmother keeps telling you that you resemble your great aunt Bertha or your French teacher continues to call you by your older sister's name). You are an individual unlike anyone else. You are as good as anyone and better than no one. No matter who you are, or where you are in life, YOU have something to offer everyone.

Your Good Posture

The basis of all this poise and confidence is "good posture." Aha, I caught you squirming to sit up straight, right? That's OK everyone does this when I mention posture. Another tip, the military, stiff way you are probably holding your shoulders right now is not good posture. Good posture, more than anything, is a comfortable feeling. In fact, by the time you finish this chapter and really get into good posture you will find it very uncomfortable to stand with any other posture.

You can do EVERYTHING better with good posture. Why? Here are three basic reasons why good posture is important:

1 ➤ Health   When you have good posture, all of your organs do what they're supposed to do. You breathe better, speak better, FEEL better.

2 ➤ Appearance   A young girl will look her BEST when she has good posture. She will look sophisticated.

3 ➤ Confidence   The wonderful feeling we just discussed.

Experiment

Try this experiment sometime. Take a beautiful, possibly expensive new dress and put it on a girl with poor posture. That dress will look horrible. Now put an ugly, inexpensive, old dress on a girl with good posture. That dress will look great. Try it and see for yourself what a difference good posture makes.

The way you carry yourself will tell others whether you are an energetic, tired, positive or negative person. Posture affects your image as others see you *and* as you see yourself. It reflects your personality, confidence, and attitude.

How Do You Get Good Posture?

You must be eager to get into the "nitty gritty" of good posture, so here it is to have and to hold forever. It's not easy. You must practice daily. Strive for good posture. For some reason, tall girls feel they have to be short, that they won't be as noticed if they slouch. You will be noticed when you slouch, but it will not be the same attention you will receive with good posture.

A true story I have to share with you goes back many years to my days in finishing school. There was a tall, not very pretty, extremely round-shouldered young lady who started classes. Well, by the time she completed her course, she was still tall, not very pretty but most attractive with beautiful posture. She went on to become an instructor and was the perfect example of "before" and "after" good posture. Whenever she would walk into a room heads would turn and you could hear mumbling about how attractive she was. She took it one step further and always wore large hats, which drew more attention to her height. She didn't care how tall she was because she had perfect posture and was most confident.

Building Blocks

Imagine your body being divided into three building blocks; one directly on top of the other. Or a strand of pearls with one pearl directly on top of the other. If you could peek inside your body, what you would see is a spine as straight as a skeleton's.

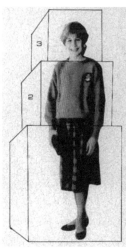

- ☛ Your FIRST building block is from your FEET TO YOUR HIPS. Weight should be evenly distributed which means the exact same amount on each foot. Knees are neither bent nor locked, just a slight flex. ▶

- ☛ Your SECOND building block is from your HIPS TO YOUR SHOULDERS. Hips are tucked under. Tummy is held in nice and tight. Imagine your belly button meeting your spine. Rib cage is lifted. Don't stick it out so your back is arched. Shoulders are low and broad, lined up with ears. They will relax in this position and not be stiff and rigid.

- ☛ Your THIRD building block is your HEAD and is the very hardest to hold straight. Your chin should be parallel to the floor as if it's resting on a shelf and head centered over your shoulders, not forward like an ostrich. Keep your nose in the air at a friendly angle.

In my classes I mention to my students that nothing good, diamonds, candy, or money, is ever thrown on the floor. Therefore, there's never a need to look down. Glance down with your eyes only, not your head. Imagine a big pink helium-filled balloon attached to the top of your head. The shiny balloon is pulling your body up, stretching the spinal cord and lifting your neck up and away from your body.

Posture Check

- 👉 Get ready — Put on a pair of leotards or swim suit.
- 👉 Get set — Place yourself before a full length mirror.
- 👉 GO — For a posture check...

Feet	pointed straight ahead, weight balanced on both
Knees	slightly flexed; not relaxed and not stiff
Derriere	tucked under nice and tight. Squeeze.
Waist	pulled up, up, up and out of hips
Rib cage	lifted but not out so your back arches
Shoulders	low and broad; lined up with your ears
Neck	pulled back, up and out of shoulders
Chin	pretend it's sitting on a shelf
Head	centered over your shoulders

Are you lined up properly or are you not quite with it yet? You will be soon because you are the proud owner of a series of wonderful, guaranteed to cure poor posture, exercises. There are reasons for poor posture such as laziness, overstuffed chairs, excessive weight, poor mattress, foot problems or improper shoes to mention a few, but why focus on the negative, when you have the positive right here. POSTURE

Exercises

Rag Doll: Place your derriere against a wall, heels about a foot away from the wall. Bend over at the waist and fall like a rag doll; very loose and limber, all the way to the floor. (See photos at right, opposite page. ▶)

Slowly raise torso, pressing spine against the wall. There should be no space between the small of your back, which is your spine, and the wall. Check with your hand to see. Now slide down the wall. If your spine starts to come away from the wall, STOP and start all over again. After you have slid down the wall, come up with the small of your back still pressed against the wall.

This exercise is a daily must and will correct a sway back.

Hold Up: Stay in the same finished position above. This time you are going to use only your arms. Your elbows and backs of your hands are flat against the wall, as if you were being "held up." Extend your arms above your head while at the same time keeping them flat against the wall. You will feel a pull or slight strain with this one. Great for rounded shoulders.

Shoulder Roll: This one you've done many times already. Check your posture and now roll your shoulders forward, up as though you are trying to touch your earlobes, lower them.

Head Roll: Another exercise you have probably done in dance class or at some other time. Your head is centered over your shoulders. Keep your chin parallel to the floor and move your head over your right shoulder. Drop your head back and move it over your left shoulder. Return to center. Reverse. (See photos, below. ▼)

Book Walk: Sure, try walking with a book on your head. This is also referred to as models' posture. If it stays on you're on your way. Keep up the good work! Should it tumble down, don't despair, pick it up and try, try again. Now repeat your posture check. Doesn't your waist look slimmer? Don't you feel a little bit taller? And I KNOW you feel better. That's good posture.

Once you have acquired good posture, it will feel awkward and uncomfortable to stand any other way.

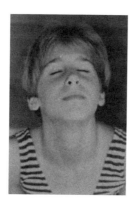

Correct Stance

Standing is a big part of your life. Just think how often you have to stand. You stand and wait for the school bus and rides. You stand in the lunch line. You stand between classes, at parties. The list goes on and on.

Luckily, there is a proper way to stand. A way that is comfortable, natural and pretty. Haven't you noticed the way models stand, television personalities, Miss America contestants, all so pretty and poised.

There is no official name for the basic stance, but it has been referred to as a hesitation, basic foot position or even a model-t position.

It's quite simple. Imagine you are standing in the center of a large clock, with both feet together and pointing straight ahead to 12 o'clock. Pick up your right toe and point it to 2 o'clock. Pick up your entire left foot and point it to 12 o'clock. The heel of your left foot should be at the instep of your right foot. This is called a *left* basic foot position because your left foot is in the front.

left basic

◀ For a *right* basic foot position, reverse the stance. Stand with your feet together and imagine you are still in the center of the clock. Pick up your left toe and point it to 10 o'clock. Now, pick up your entire right foot and point it to 12 o'clock. Again the front foot is straight ahead and the back foot is pointed at about a 45 degree angle. This is a right basic foot position because your right foot is the front foot. It doesn't matter which foot is in the front, what does make a difference is that you stand in a basic foot position. Let it become a natural way of standing with you, then you won't feel like everyone is staring at you and it will give you confidence to know you look your prettiest while standing.

right basic

Practice in front of a mirror. Ask someone in your family to take a picture of you standing properly.

Oh, and what to do with your hands? Let them fall gracefully from your shoulders. Have one hand slightly in front; the other slightly in back. There is nothing pretty about knuckles, therefore, keep your fingers in profile.

Sitting Properly

Decide where you would like to sit before you rush into a room and "plop" down on a chair. Approach your chair with confidence. That chair is just waiting for YOU.

While standing in your basic foot position, be sure the calf of your back leg is touching the chair. Sit on the edge of your chair and slide back onto the chair. Use your knuckles if you need a little help. Angle your body just a little bit in the direction of your basic foot position.

Foot Positions

Your feet should still be in a basic foot position. Choose one of these pretty and comfortable ways of placing your feet.

Basic Foot Position — Just the way you are

Ankle Cross — Tuck your back foot around your front foot crossing ankles (prettiest)

Ankle Cross Tilt — Same as above, but tilt your feet to the side (same side as basic foot position) ▶

Avoid: Crossing your legs, swinging your feet, pointing or tapping your toes on the floor, wrapping your heel around the leg of the chair, putting your feet on the furniture or taking your shoes off...

Hand Positions

When your hands are in a correct position, it shows you are poised, interested and confident!

Palms Up	One palm in the other; both facing upward
Palms together	Bottom palm up; top palm down
Laced Fingers	Simply lace your fingers

If you keep your hands on one thigh or the other, it will look even prettier.

Avoid: Playing with jewelry, chewing on or tapping your fingers, picking at your face or fiddling with your hair.

Rising

You sat gracefully, so now you must get up the same way! Be certain that your feet are in their basic foot position or you might fall. I don't teach how to fall gracefully! Use your hands if necessary, slide to the edge of your chair and rise. Of course, you are standing nice and straight! Keep practicing. In school, you might be required to sit "Indian style" and you have to obey your teacher. However, any other time a lady always sits with her knees together...

Graceful Walk

Begin walking with your front foot. (Aren't you still standing in your basic foot position? I thought you were.) If anyone has ever said to you, "I could tell it was you, I could tell by your walk." Don't take it as a compliment. Think about someone whose walk is quite noticeable. How do you recognize it? It's probably a loud clomp, clomp, clomp.

Just a couple of things to remember about walking without getting too technical. Try to keep your toes pointed straight ahead rather than toeing in or out. If you will bring your entire foot down at one time you will never hear the famous "heel, toe clomp"

The size of your step should be about the size of your foot. In a hurry? Don't take giant steps, just take more. Swing your arms gently from your shoulders, not your elbows.

Many years ago, a new neighbor of mine was unaware that I taught finishing school. One day it came up in a conversation so I told her what I did. Well, with that she became very excited and said that explained why I walk funny. I continued and pointed out that she was one who was walking funny. We still laugh about that. A poised, graceful walk is noticed but unheard.

Etcetera

What is a Pivot?

A pivot is merely a graceful way of turning. Models pivot on the runway. You probably pivot many times during the day without even realizing it. You just think you're turning.

Stand in your basic foot position and step out with your front foot. Now with your back foot, step in front of your other foot. Pick up your heels and turn on the balls of your feet in the direction of your back foot. As you practice say, "step, step, turn."

This is called a half pivot. Repeat what you have just one in order to complete your turn. Now you have done a full pivot. You should be right back where you started.

Handbags

A shoulder bag is carried on your shoulder. The handle doesn't swing to a beat as you walk.

A clutch bag is carried down at your side. Never under your armpit.

A tote or large bag is held by the handle and carried down at your side.

A backpack is carried on your back.

Stairs

When you go up the stairs, place your entire foot on the step. Do not permit your heel to hang off because this can be dangerous. If you need to hold on to the railing, by all means do so. Your head does not bob up and down either.

Coats

As usual, you want a poised, coordinated look when you put on and remove your coat, whether you are alone or in the presence of others. The rule here is not to be in the way of others. Watch out for objects on tables, counters, shelves. Avoid swinging or flinging your coat. Keep it close to your body. Button from the top down. Unbutton from the bottom up.

To carry your coat, put the sleeves together, fold them under and carry the smooth edge out.

Gloves

Gloves are not necessarily just for warmth but can by stylish as well. Hold your glove at the base and put all your fingers in at the same time. To remove, grasp all fingers at the same time and one pull will do it. Avoid, the milking cow look you get when you pull each finger separately. Put your thumbs together and hold the fingers in your hand when carrying your gloves. Better yet, put them in your purse or coat pocket so they won't get lost.

Friendship

CHAPTER TEN

To Have A Friend, You Must Be A Friend

Students have shared with me their thoughts on friendship. What does friendship mean to you?

Friendship means to be nice, caring, giving and sharing. To understand and to be there in need.

Friendship means that she is always kind, helps you when you're in trouble, doesn't force you to do something you don't want to do and is kind to other people.

A friend doesn't get mad when you ask someone else over and doesn't leave you alone when you're sad.

A friend is someone who is there for you when you need someone to talk to.

A friend is trustworthy and can keep a real private secret.

A friend is someone you like a lot and who understands you.

A friend is someone who listens to your joys and misfortunes because she likes you not because she wants something from you.

A friend cares about your feelings.

A friend likes you for who you are, not for what you have.

A friend is the best thing in the world.

A friend is someone who is with you for all times and will be your friend no matter what becomes of either of you.

A friend is someone who will always, always be your friend.

A friend is a very special someone.

A friend is someone to trust, to depend on and to share your feelings with.

A friend would not do anything to try to aggravate you.

A friend is nice.

A friend knows all about you and still loves you.

Friendship means not calling people names or not liking them for what's on the outside. It's the inside that counts.

Friendship is a special thing. Friendship means that you wouldn't want your friend to be hurt or sad. You want her to be happy because when your friend is happy you are happy. You share things with your friend, invite her over and love your friend in a special way.

Friendship is when people don't call you names just because you are a little overweight.

Friendship is when people help you through the good and the bad.

Friendship is when people don't hurt you with words, hands or feet.

Friendship means sharing, loving and caring.

Friendship means having fun. It means liking someone.

A friend is a present you give yourself.

Friendship is the most important thing in life because you always need a friend...

Parting Words

Remember always that "kindness to others" whether at home, at school or at play is the basis of all social etiquette. Don't worry about memorizing a lot of rules. The only real rule to consider is the *Golden Rule.*

Real beauty begins "within." Think of a tiny rosebud beginning to open and soon blossoming radiantly into a beautiful flower. As you grow and develop poise and confidence you, too, will blossom into a radiant young lady. Good manners will always have their rewards.

If you have enjoyed this book or I can ever help you in any way, please feel free to drop me a note...

The fun I have had in writing and rewriting the Pretty As A Picture book has come to an end; however, this is just the beginning for Y-O-U!

Maria Everding
The Etiquette Institute
12973 Fiddle Creek Lane
Saint Louis, Missouri 63131